Linda McCartney's World of Vegetarian Cooking

Linda McCartney's World of Vegetarian Cooking

Over 200 Meat-Free Dishes from Around the World

Linda McCartney

Photographer
Debbie Patterson

Food Consultant
Rosamond Richardson

Home Economist
Jane Suthering

A Bulfinch Press Book
Little, Brown and Company
Boston • New York • London

I dedicate this book to my delicious family, who are everything to me.

Like all diets, a vegetarian diet should be a balanced one. If you have any doubts or concerns about whether your diet is suitable, you should consult your doctor. Additionally, if you have allergies, you should not use those recipes that contain ingredients to which you may be allergic or otherwise affected.

Some recipes in this book contain raw eggs. It is advisable that these are not served to the young, elderly, or pregnant.

Published in hardcover as *Linda McCartney on Tour,* 1998
First paperback edition, 2001

ISBN 0-8212-2487-5 (hc) / ISBN 0-8212-2696-7 (pb)

Library of Congress Control Number 98-17947

Food stylist: Jane Suthering
Prop stylist: Tessa Evelegh
Designer: Janet James
Editorial team: Julia Charles, Mary McCartney, Louise Morris, Sue Prochnik, Elaine Steer
Americanization: Arianne Burnette

Published simultaneously in the United States of America by Bulfinch Press, an imprint and trademark of Little, Brown and Company (Inc.), in Great Britain by Little, Brown and Company (UK)

The author would like to thank Paul, Heather, Stella, Mary, James, Louise, Sue, Elaine, Helge, Pat, Alistair, Robby and team, Bo, Roger, Joanne, Dav, Kim, Fred, Nick, Monique, Laura and Donald, Shelagh, Marie, Tim and team, Julia and team, Carol Judy and team, John and Louise, Zoë and Elizabeth and everyone who helped and shared a veggie recipe

Printed and bound in the U.S.A.

Contents

V INDICATES A VEGAN DISH

Vegetarianism is now the biggest food trend of the century and I, for one, couldn't be more thrilled! Since I wrote my previous cookbooks more and more people have taken responsibility for their health and their planet by adopting a meat-free diet—at the present growth rate it is predicted that we will ALL be veggie by the year 2050, so if you don't want to be left behind now is the time to get started!

If you are still considering your choices and need a little more encouragement, take time to think about the following facts for a minute or two. Recent statistics have revealed that a life-long non-meat-eater saves about 760 chickens, 5 cows, 20 pigs, 29 sheep, 46 turkeys, 7 rabbits, and over half a ton of fish. Just imagine standing in a farm and looking at all these lives that you, as a meat-eater, will indirectly have ended in your own lifetime! I can't think of a more literal and convincing argument, and nothing outweighs the rewards of living a guilt-free and compassionate life.

Another important factor that has no doubt contributed to the boom in the number of new veggies is meat poisoning. This has been one of the biggest political and social issues of recent years—with the alarming increase in cases of BSE and CJD, eating meat has become a risky business. There is really no need to take any risks with your health in our modern and civilized society, and you reserve the right to eat food that is clean and pure. Curiously, many people still believe that their health will suffer if they cut meat out of their diet; most doctors and nutritionists would not agree.

Today, more than ever before, becoming a veggie is one of the easiest and most positive decisions you can make. You will be spoilt for choice in shops and restaurants and, thanks to the wonders of modern food technology, even the traditional meat-eater who loves burgers, sausages, and bacon no longer has to make any sacrifices.

As you can see, there are many good reasons to go veggie, but I've been saving one of the best until last and that is that meat-free food is delicious! It is exciting and modern. What I'm aiming to show you in this book is that cutting out meat doesn't mean leaving just the veg—it's about learning a different way of cooking and adopting a whole new approach to the way that you choose to feed yourself. The first thing you'll discover as you start following my recipes is your tastebuds—there's a whole world of flavors out there! I've included many of my favorite dishes from around the world—memorable meals that I've enjoyed with family and friends over the years—on holiday as well as at work. The more I've researched this book, the more I have come to realize how much we can learn by looking at other cultures where meat and dairy products have never been plentiful (or for religious reasons not widely eaten) and how, with a little creative use of herbs, spices, and exotic ingredients, meat-free feasts can be created from the simplest of foods.

Even if you find cooking a little daunting, my new collection of recipes is guaranteed to bring out the cook in you. Don't be afraid to adapt my recipes to suit your own tastes and remember that veggie cooking is all about having fun, being creative, and doing something not just for yourself but for your planet and the animals you share it with.

Linda McCartney
April 1998

Nutrition for Vegetarians

What is a vegetarian?

Even though all the surveys tell us that the number of vegetarians and non-meat-eaters is growing by leaps and bounds, many people still do not really know what being a vegetarian means. This is partly because there are a number of different kinds—demi-veggies, lacto/ovo veggies, and vegans are the main three. A true veggie will not eat any food that is, or contains, the flesh of any animal, bird, or fish. Nor will they eat anything that has been made from any body part of an animal, bird, or fish. This could be lard or suet (made from animal fat), gelatin (made from animal bones, hooves, and hide, or fish bones), rennet in cheese (it can be made from calves' stomachs), finings used to clear wine (can be made from egg or gelatin), some additives that can be derived from animal fats, or vitamin or mineral supplements in gelatin casings. However, vegetarians will eat animal produce—eggs or dairy products that may come from animals but are not actually part of their bodies. These vegetarians are also known as "lacto (milk)/ovo (egg) vegetarians".

Vegans, on the other hand, will not eat anything that has come from an animal at all. Many maintain that if you do not eat animals themselves, then it is not logical to eat anything that comes from an animal, such as milk and dairy products, eggs, and honey.

Vegetarian nutrition

Even though so many people are now reducing the amount of meat they eat or switching to a vegetarian or demi-veg diet, some people (parents especially) are still worried that a vegetarian or vegan diet can't provide all the nourishment that a body needs to remain healthy. This couldn't be further from the truth. A well-balanced meat-free diet is now widely regarded to be the healthiest choice. So let us look at the nutrients in turn. (For a more detailed guide to nutrient sources, see the chart on pages 12 and 13.)

Protein

Most people in the Western world eat nearly twice as much protein as they actually need. Beans, nuts, and seeds are all good sources of protein, although the best, from a vegetarian point of view, is soy, because it is the only non-animal food that contains all the amino acids. In "nutrition speak" it is a "complete protein."

Carbohydrates

Starchy carbohydrate foods (known as complex carbohydrates) are the basis of a balanced diet and vegetarian food has loads of them. Cereals, grains, beans, and root vegetables are widely used in many vegetarian dishes, so there are no worries there.

Fats

Most people are concerned about eating too much fat, not too little. Vegetarians are one step ahead here, as they have cut out a number of "saturated" animal fats. However, cheese and milk-eating vegetarians need to keep an eye on their general dairy intake. It is a great temptation to fill up on cheese, yogurt, and other milk-based foods, some of which have a very high fat content.

Fiber

Unlike fat, most people tend to eat too little rather than too much fiber, but here again vegetarians are ahead, as those eating lots of starchy carbohydrates (see left) will automatically be getting a good daily intake of fiber.

Vitamins and minerals

Most vegetarian foods are a good source of vitamins and minerals.

Calcium is the mineral that is of most concern to vegans who do not eat dairy products. However, tofu (soybean curd) is a rich source of calcium, as are green leafy vegetables. Many soy milks are also fortified with extra calcium. Iron is also to be found in tofu, beans, green leafy vegetables, and dried fruits such as prunes and apricots.

Wheat germ, wholegrain cereals, legumes, soy, nuts, seeds, and seaweed, all widely used in vegetarian cooking, are all good sources of chromium, copper, iodine, magnesium, manganese, molybdenum, phosphorus, potassium, selenium, and zinc, so vegetarians need have no concerns about going short on minerals!

Shopping for vegetarian foods

Vegetarian shopping is no different from any other shopping if you are just buying raw materials such as fruits, vegetables, or legumes. It becomes just a little bit harder when you buy prepared products—from mayonnaise to full meals. Many composite dishes use animal products in their ingredients, but if you do not read the label carefully—and knowledgeably—you may not realize this.

Reading labels

Beware of hidden ingredients. Once you are used to reading labels and have memorized some of the most important ingredients, recognizing animal ingredients will become second nature when you shop.

Animal fats

These are used in lots of products, both food and household. Cookies, crackers, and cakes often contain animal fats, so unless the label specifies "vegetable fats" do not buy them. Check the labels on pastry products too—the pastry is usually made with vegetable fat, but not always.

Spreads

Check the ingredients lists carefully before you buy your spread. Many include dairy products (whey or casein) that will not be a problem if you are vegetarian, but will if you are vegan.

Make sure that you buy non-hydrogenated spreads. Although hydrogenation does not involve animal products, it is a process by which vegetable oils are heated to a very high temperature so that they harden and can be used as spreads. Unfortunately the changes in the oil caused by this process make it much more difficult for the body to absorb the fat and may even harm our bodies.

Rennet

Rennet is what separates the curds from the whey in cheesemaking and it used to be made from the lining of calves' stomachs. In fact, the majority of cheesemakers today use a vegetable-based rennet, but you can't be sure unless it specifies "vegetable rennet" on the package.

Gelatin or jelling agents

Most gelatin is made from animals hides, hooves, and bones and from fish bones. Gelatin crops up in all kinds of products, savory and, especially, sweet, so check all prepared desserts and yogurts.

If you take vitamin supplements, you should also check whether the capsules have been made from gelatin—there are vegetarian equivalents. And check the source of the vitamin itself as several have animal derivations.

Additives

Take care over emulsifiers E470 to E479. They are made from fatty acids that can be of animal or vegetable origin but they rarely tell you which.

Dairy products and eggs

These will not be a problem if you are vegetarian, but if you are vegan and need to avoid them you have some more learning to do. Dairy and egg products are very widely used in food manufacture, so watch out for any of the following:

Dairy:	Eggs:
Casein/caseinates	Albumin/conalbumin or ovalbumin
Ghee	Ovomucoid/ovoglobulin
Lactose	Vitellin/vitellenin
Whey	

Sauces and stocks

You need to check the labels carefully on prepared sauces and stocks. Some have very obvious animal ingredients. Others, such as mayonnaise (eggs) or Worcestershire sauce (anchovies), may not be so clear.

prepared foods

As the number of vegetarians grows, so does the range of meat-free foods on offer to us—especially prepared foods. Many major manufacturers now produce vegetarian versions of all the standard dishes, such as lasagna or chili. Others make vegetarian burgers and sausages, and of course my own range of meat-free meals is expanding all the time. Many Indian, Chinese, or Far Eastern dishes will also be vegetarian, but unless it is a vegetarian product line, you should still check the label carefully.

Alternatives to dairy products

For many years, if you did not want to eat dairy products, all you were offered was rather "chalky" tasting soy milk. However, things are a lot better today.

Soy milks and yogurts now come in a wide range of flavors, they are fortified with vitamins and minerals, and organic brands are available. Soy cream, which tastes not unlike real cream and is excellent in cooked dishes, as well as on desserts, is now available too. Tofu (soybean curd) can be found soft (silken) or set like a cheese, and you can buy it plain, smoked, or marinated. It is excellent in a wide range of casseroles, stir-fries, salads, and sandwiches.

Textured Vegetable Protein, or TVP, uses soy to create a meat-type product that is often almost indistinguishable from the real thing and is excellent for those many vegetarians who actually like the texture and taste of meat but do not like the idea of eating it.

Meanwhile, medical research suggests that soy is an excellent food to eat to protect you against a whole range of other twentieth-century diseases.

And for those who do not actually like the taste of soy milk as a drink or on their breakfast cereal, you can now also buy rice milk (sweet but pleasant) and oat milk. For cooking, coconut milk (which can be bought canned or made by boiling desiccated coconut in water) is also excellent.

Organic produce and foods

Eating organic food is one of the most important contributions any of us can make to save the planet. Over 25,000 tons of pesticides, herbicides, and fungicides are used in Britain alone every year.

In one sense, all food is "organic" because it has come from plants or animals. However, for the past fifty years or so, "organic" has been used specifically to describe food grown without artificial fertilizers or pesticides and in a way that produces optimum quantities of food of high nutritional quality with minimal damage to the environment and wildlife. The term "organic" is now protected by European Community law and it means that the product has been rigorously inspected from the farm to the shop by an independent control body, such as the Soil Association in the UK.

Organic farmers and producers employ cultivation and crop rotation systems in order to develop natural soil fertility. This means that the soil is enriched by composted manures, nitrogen-fixing plants, and naturally occurring minerals, rather than by artificial fertilizers. In addition, trees, hedgerows, and field boundaries are planted and managed to prevent soil erosion and to encourage wildlife, which in turn encourages natural pest control and alleviates the need for toxic pesticides. Dairy products or eggs marked organic are provided by animals fed on organic grass, fodder, or grain, who have not been intensively farmed or injected with growth hormones or antibiotics.

Because it is not farmed intensively and because organic farmers are more interested in the health of their crops than getting every apple exactly the same shape as every other apple, organic fruits and vegetables may not look as perfect as non-organic—but they often taste a lot better!

Because organic farming is more labor intensive, there are still a relatively small number of organic farmers, and because the industry is not well subsidized, organic produce can still be appreciably more expensive than ordinary produce, although prices are now starting to come down. Potatoes, carrots, and onions are fairly cheap and are a good way to test how much better organic food tastes.

If your local health food store or supermarket doesn't stock organic produce, ask them for it. Supply creates demand and there is no better way to support the organic movement.

Eating out

There are very few restaurants now that do not offer some kind of vegetarian alternative. And you do not need to feel awkward about asking for it, as many people who are not veggies choose the vegetarian alternative as a lighter, healthier option. However, it is still worth checking whether sauces, pastries, and desserts have been made with vegetarian ingredients (no meat stocks, no animal fats, no gelatin).

But once again, if you are a vegan, you need to be more careful because you can't eat anything that has been cooked with butter, cream, cheese, yogurt, eggs, or honey.

If you are going to a meat-eating friend's home to eat, give them ample warning and let them rise to the challenge—you can always offer a few suggestions of your own.

Eating in

Meat eaters often claim that cooking vegetarian food is much harder than cooking meat-based food, but I can't think why. It is no more difficult to cook a veggie loaf and some side dishes than it is to cook roast beef and two vegetables! If you are having meat-eating friends over for a meal, you don't think twice before serving them vegetarian food. There are so many delicious and exciting recipes for non-meat dishes in this book alone that the chances are that they will not even notice that they haven't eaten any meat!

The vegetarian pantry

As any good cook knows, a well stocked pantry is a great way to start.

Beans and legumes

Split peas, whole lentils, and split lentils do not need to be soaked overnight, but it is recommended that you soak the other legumes for approximately 8–12 hours. The times given below are a rough guide, as cooking times can vary considerably depending on the age and origin of the crop. The first ten minutes' cooking of all except lentils and split peas should be done at a fast boil, uncovered, to destroy any toxic elements on the outer skin, except soybeans, which should boil hard for the first hour. Although lentils and split peas do not need to be soaked overnight, they will cook faster if they are first steeped in boiling water for 15–30 minutes. Drain them before cooking.

Once cooked, beans, peas, and lentils keep well for several days in a covered container in the refrigerator, or they can be frozen and will still retain their flavor. Cool and open-freeze them, then pack them in rigid containers and label them. For soups, a handful or two can be removed and put straight into the soup near the end of the cooking time. For salads, allow them to thaw for about an hour at room temperature or overnight in the refrigerator.

Adzuki beans	45 minutes
Black-eyed peas	45–50 minutes
Black beans	50–60 minutes
Broad or fava beans	1½ hours
Butter or lima beans	60–90 minutes
Cannellini or white kidney beans	45–50 minutes
Flageolets	45–50 minutes
Haricot or navy beans	50–60 minutes
Mung beans	30–45 minutes
Pinto beans	60–90 minutes
Red kidney beans	45–50 minutes
Soybeans	2–2½ hours
Chickpeas or garbanzo beans	60–90 minutes
Whole green peas	60–90 minutes
Split peas	40–45 minutes
Whole lentils	30–45 minutes
Split lentils	15–30 minutes

Soy products

Soybeans are immensely useful to the vegetarian. Not only do they provide soy milk (made by boiling soybeans in water, then straining it) and soy cream (made from soy milk), but tofu (soybean curd), tempeh, miso, soy sauce, and tamari (all seasonings or sauce made from fermented soybeans), soy margarine and oil (both healthy fats for cooking and spreading), soy flour (widely used in baking), and TVP, or textured vegetable protein, which is used to provide the majority of "meat" substitutes. TVP comes both chilled and frozen and can be used straight from the fridge or freezer. Other meat substitutes are made from wheat gluten or a myco-protein, which is mushroom in origin, and are very successful. Use them as you would TVP.

Soy milk and cream both come in Long Life versions and there are dozens of different flavors of soy milk suitable for both drinking and cooking.

Tofu comes in soft (silken) or set textures and in a variety of flavors and can be added to casseroles, salads, and many ethnic dishes.

Nuts and seeds

Always keep a good stock of nuts (almonds, brazil nuts, cashews, hazelnuts, pecans, peanuts, pine nuts, pistachios, walnuts). They can be added to almost any vegetarian dish, either whole or crushed, as they are or toasted. Not only do they add lots of flavor and texture to the dish, but also plenty of vitamins and minerals. However, they are also very calorific!

Seeds (pumpkin, sunflower, poppy, sesame) are equally useful for adding flavor and texture. Being lower in fat, they are just as nutritious but not as calorific as nuts.

Fruit and vegetables

The other mainstay of the vegetarian diet should be fresh fruits and vegetables, ideally organic (see page 10). Root vegetables are wonderfully filling and keep very well. Most vegetables are excellent either cooked or raw and are extremely nutritious. Fresh fruits can be used fresh or cooked, on their own or in desserts.

Although fresh organic fruit and vegetables are ideal, it is well worth keeping some canned and dried stocks in the cupboard for emergencies.

Canned tomatoes are invaluable in any casserole, stew, or sauce, while canned corn, pimientos, artichoke hearts, and olives make excellent and flavorsome additions to any vegetarian dish.

Dried fruits (raisins, currants, prunes, apricots, figs) are great as snacks or mixed with fresh fruits in a dessert or in cakes and baked goods.

Protein

Proteins are made up of amino acids, and different foods contain different amino acids. The foods listed below are all good sources of protein, although soy is the best because it contains all the amino acids that we need.

GOOD SOURCES

* *Soy products*—soy milk, tofu, and TVP
* *Beans, peas & lentils*
* *Cereals & whole grains*—rice, oatmeal, wholewheat flour
* *Nuts & seeds*—including dishes made from nuts and seeds, i.e. tahini, hummus
* *Dairy products*—milk, butter, cheese
* *Eggs*

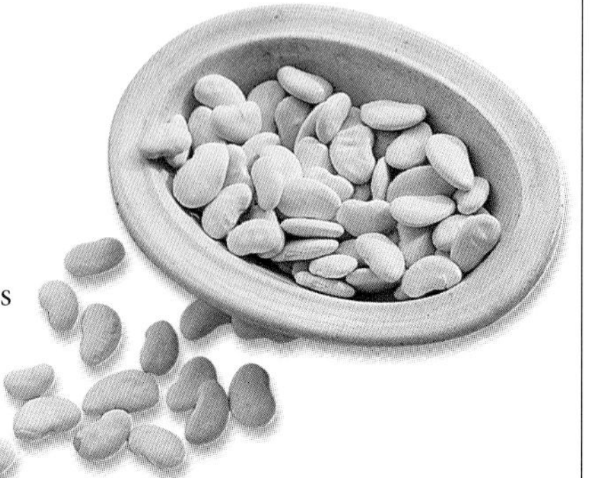

Fat

A certain amount of fat is absolutely essential to allow your body to function properly but it must be the right kind of fat. Fats fall into three main categories.

Saturated fats. These can be bad for us if we eat too much of them, as they convert into cholesterol in our bodies, which can lead to heart disease. Saturated fats come mainly from animal foods, whole milk, butter, hard cheese, and some nuts.

Polyunsaturated and **monounsaturated fats** provide essential fatty acids that the body needs. (Polyunsaturated fats come from liquid oils and are sometimes "hydrogenated". However, the hydrogenation changes the nature of the fat so that the body can't use it in the same way as a normal polyunsaturated fat.)

GOOD SOURCES

* *Cold pressed vegetable oils*—olive, sunflower, soy, corn
* *Non-hydrogenated spreads & margarines*
* *Nuts*
* *Avocados*

Carbohydrates

Starchy carbohydrate foods (known as complex carbohydrates) are the basis of a balanced diet.

Sugary carbohydrate foods (known as simple carbohydrates) have little nutritional value and lots of calories, and should be avoided. They are in sugar, candy, chocolate, and cakes and cookies made with refined flours and sugars.

GOOD SOURCES

* *Beans, peas & lentils*
* *Whole grains, rices & cereals**
* *Pasta*
* *Most fresh fruit & vegetables*—especially potatoes, root vegetables & bananas

Fiber

Fiber is to be found in complex carbohydrates and is important for helping waste to pass rapidly through the digestive system.

GOOD SOURCES

* *Beans, peas & lentils*
* *Oats*
* *Dried fruits*
* *Whole grains & wholemeal cereals*
* *Virtually all fresh fruits & vegetables*—especially berries, carrots & cabbage

Vitamins

Our bodies need a small amount of each vitamin to function properly, but except for Vitamin D (which the body can manufacture itself from sunlight) they cannot make their own vitamins, so we need to get them from the food we eat.

VITAMIN A

Needed for healthy skin and good vision.

GOOD SOURCES

* *Carrots*
* *Broccoli*
* *Green leafy vegetables*
* *Red & yellow bell peppers*
* *Dried apricots*
* *Melons & mangoes*
* *Dairy products*

B VITAMINS

8 different B vitamins help to release energy and essential nutrients.

GOOD SOURCES

* *Whole grain cereals*
* *Yeast extract*
* *Nuts & seeds*
* *Wide range of fruits & vegetables*—especially green vegetables, mushrooms, bananas & avocados

VITAMIN B12

Needed for the formation of red blood cells and genetic material and protection of the nerves.

GOOD SOURCES

* *Yeast extract*
* *Seaweeds & alfalfa sprouts*
* *Fortified soy milk, margarine & breakfast cereals*
* *Fermented soy foods*—soy sauce, miso, tamari

Vitamin C

Essential for the formation and maintenance of bones, teeth, and tissue and for overall health. Since we can't store Vitamin C in our bodies, we need to eat Vitamin C-bearing foods on a daily basis. Vitamin C is destroyed by light and heat, so it is better to eat at least some of your fruits and vegetables raw.

Good sources

* *Citrus & berry fruits*
* *Kiwi fruit*
* *Red bell peppers*
* *Potatoes*
* *Tomatoes*

Vitamin D

Needed for the absorption of calcium into the body. Vitamin D is manufactured by the body when exposed to sunlight, but it can also be found in some foods.

Good sources

* *Eggs*
* *Fortified cereals*
* *Fortified margarine*

Vitamin E

Needed for red blood cell formation, general healing, and to protect the body against the harmful effects of free radicals.

Good sources

* *Nuts & seeds*
* *Vegetables oils & spreads*
* *Wheat germ & whole grain cereals*
* *Avocados*

Vitamin K

Vitamin K is needed for blood clotting and bone health, but at least half of our daily needs are manufactured by the body itself.

Good sources

* *Green leafy vegetables*
* *Seaweeds*
* *Carrots*

Folic acid

Folic acid works alongside vitamin 12 to form new cells, in particular those in our bone marrow that produce red and white blood cells. Research has suggested that it has a role to play in preventing birth defects such as spina bifida and pregnant women should increase their intake of folic acid-rich foods.

Good sources

* *Yeast extract*
* *Wheat germ*
* *Nuts*—especially peanuts
* *Beans, peas & legumes*
* *Fortified breakfast cereals*
* *Green leafy vegetables*—especially spinach, broccoli, cabbage

Minerals

Iron

Iron is essential for the formation of red blood cells and the functioning of several enzymes in the body.

Good sources

* *Tofu*
* *Beans & legumes*
* *Nuts & seeds*
* *Green leafy vegetables*
* *Dried fruits*—apricots, prunes
* *Blackstrap molasses*
* *Wheat germ and wholemeal cereals*

Calcium

Calcium is essential for the growth and maintenance of bones and for controlling nerve impulses to and from the brain.

Good sources

* *Tofu*
* *Dairy products*
* *Fortified soy products*
* *Green leafy vegetables*—especially watercress
* *Okra*
* *Nuts*—especially almonds and brazils
* *Dried fruits*—figs, apricots

Zinc

Zinc is vital for the functioning of the body, especially the immune system and resistance to infection.

Good sources

* *Dairy products*
* *Nuts & seeds*—pumpkin & sesame
* *Whole grains, cereals & rice*
* *Wheat germ*
* *Legumes*—lentils

Iodine

Essential for many metabolic functions, especially the proper functioning of the thyroid gland.

Good sources

* *Seaweeds*
* *Iodized salt*
* *Green leafy vegetables*

Magnesium

Needed for normal calcium function. It is also used in every cell in our bodies and to enable some enzymes needed for energy to function properly.

Good sources

* *Whole grain cereals & wheat germ*
* *Soy products*
* *Tofu*
* *Nuts & seeds*
* *Green leafy vegetables*
* *Dried fruits*—figs, prunes

All the recipes in this book have been carefully tested to ensure that you get the right results but it is important to bear all of the following in mind before you begin.

Standard conversions

25g	1oz
50g	2oz
85g	3oz
115g	4oz
140g	5oz
175g	6oz
200g	7oz
225g	8oz
250g	9oz
275g	10oz
350g	12oz
400g	14oz
450g	1lb
700g	1lb 9oz
1kg	2lb 4oz

125ml	½ cup
250ml	1 cup
375ml	1½ cups
500ml	2 cups
625ml	2½ cups
750ml	3 cups
875ml	3½ cups
1000ml	4 cups
1 litre	4¾ cups

Ovens are all slightly different, so you may need to adjust the temperatures given in the recipes accordingly or use an oven thermometer for the most accurate reading. Fan-assisted ovens can cook food faster than conventional ovens. To compensate, you can reduce the temperature given in a recipe, but it is best to consult the manufacturer's handbook. Fan-assisted ovens have an even temperature throughout, but in conventional ovens the heat rises, so the top of the oven is hotter than the bottom. When a dish is cooked in the oven, always use the middle shelf.

275°F	140°C	gas 1	very slow
300°F	150°C	gas 2	very slow
325°F	160°C	gas 3	slow
350°F	180°C	gas 4	moderate
375°F	190°C	gas 5	moderate
400°F	200°C	gas 6	moderately hot
425°F	220°C	gas 7	hot
450°F	230°C	gas 8	hot
475°F	240°C	gas 9	very hot

Equipment

Buy the best tools and equipment you can afford, as it will last better and will produce better results.

- *Measuring cups:* ¼ cup, ⅓ cup, ½ cup, and 1 cup
- *Measuring spoons:* ¼ tsp, ½ tsp, 1 tsp, and 1 tbsp

Pots and pans

A heavy base is particularly important for gentle, even heat distribution. Pots and pans also need to have lids that fit tightly and sturdy handles that stay cool.

- *Saucepans:* 1–2 quart (small), 3 quart (medium), and 4 quart (large) capacity with lids
- *Non-stick frying pans:* 8 inches and 12 inches in diameter, preferably with lids
- *Casserole:* large, heavy, and flameproof, preferably cast iron coated in enamel, with a lid
- *Wok:* single, long handle and a lid
- *Steamer:* a double saucepan—the top or inner pan having holes that allow the steam to permeate around the food
- *Omelette pan:* 7 or 8 inches in diameter with curved sides
- *Crêpe pan:* with flat bottom and shallow, sloping side
- *Milk pan:* small, non-stick, with spout for pouring
- *Stockpot:* large, tall, and narrow
- *Stove-top grill pan:* ridged base

Knives

- *Chef's or cook's knife:* rigid, heavy, wide blade 8 or 10 inches long
- *Sharp knife for cutting fruit and vegetables:* blade 5 or 6 inches
- *Small knife for trimming and peeling:* blade 3½ or 4½ inches
- *Cutting boards*

Ovenware

It is a good idea to choose attractive dishes that can double as serving dishes.

- *Roasting pan*
- *Flat baking sheets*
- *Loaf pan:* 9 x 5 x 3 inches
- *Cake pan:* deep, loose-bottomed 7, 8 or 9 inches in diameter
- *Springform cake pan:* the sides open out and the bottom is loose to allow easy removal
- *Soufflé dishes or ramekins:* for individual servings
- *Layer-cake pans:* 2 x 7 inches
- *Jelly roll pon:* with shallow sides
- *Tartlet pans (individual)*
- *Large gratin dish*
- *Oval or round pie dish*

STARTERS

Crispy Vegetable Wontons V *China*

Wontons are an Oriental version of Italian ravioli. They are made using very thin wrappings or skins, which are made from wheat flour paste. They are sold in Asian supermarkets or some specialty food shops and can be kept in the refrigerator for up to five days or frozen successfully. (If you freeze them, make sure they are thoroughly defrosted before use.) Filo pastry makes a good alternative.

Preparation time:
30 minutes

Cooking time:
15 minutes

SERVES 4 (MAKES APPROXIMATELY 20 WONTONS)

1 tablespoon peanut oil
1/3 cup carrots, finely grated
1/2 cup cabbage, finely shredded
1/4 cup beansprouts
2 large cloves garlic, chopped finely
1 tablespoon soy sauce
3 tablespoons mashed tofu, or low-fat vegetarian cream cheese
pinch each of sea salt and sugar
1 teaspoon sesame oil
1/2 teaspoon black pepper
20 wonton skins or 2/3 pound filo pastry
vegetable oil for deep frying
Sweet and Sour Chili Dipping Sauce (page 146) or Garlic Dipping Sauce (page 147)

Heat a wok or large frying pan and add the oil. When it is hot, stir-fry the carrots, cabbage, beansprouts, and garlic for 1 minute. Set the vegetables aside and allow them to cool.

After they have cooled, combine the vegetables with the rest of the ingredients. Put a generous teaspoonful of the filling in the center of each wonton skin. Pull up two opposite corners, dampen the edges with a little water and pinch them together. (If you are using filo pastry, cut a double thickness into 4-inch squares, and brush lightly with water before filling them.) Bring up the other two corners, pinch them together with the first two, and seal with a little water, so that they look like small bundles.

Pour 2–3 inches of oil into a medium saucepan and place over medium to high heat. The oil is ready when a cube of bread browns immediately. Deep-fry the wontons in several batches until they are golden and crisp. Drain them on paper towels. Serve at once, with the Sweet and Sour Chili Dipping Sauce (page 146) or the Garlic Dipping Sauce (page 147).

PEELING GARLIC

Press down on the clove with the flat side of a knife blade, then pull away the burst skin.

Crispy Vegetable Wontons

Szechuan Fried Eggplant with Spicy Sauce ~ *China*

Preparation time: ***25 minutes***

Cooking time: ***15 minutes***

The cuisine of the Szechuan province in central China has been popular in the West for many years. It is associated with the spicy flavors of Szechuan peppercorns and dried red chilies, and typically uses salt, garlic and ginger, soy sauce, fiery bean paste, and fermented pickled vegetables.

SERVES 4–6

1 cup all-purpose flour
1 teaspoon baking powder
1/4 teaspoon sea salt
1 large organic egg
2 tablespoons olive oil
2/3 cup water
3 tablespoons chopped scallions
1 tablespoon finely grated fresh ginger
2 teaspoons chili bean sauce
2/3 cup vegetable stock (page 32)
1 tablespoon rice or cider vinegar
2 medium tomatoes, skinned and chopped
3 tablespoons tomato purée
2 tablespoons soy sauce
peanut oil for deep frying
1 pound eggplant, cut into slices 1 x 3 inches and 1/3 inch thick

For the batter, sift the flour with the baking powder and salt in a small bowl. Beat in the egg, then 1 tablespoon of olive oil, and finally the water. Beat until smooth. Let the batter sit for 20 minutes before using it.

Heat a wok or large frying pan and add the remaining tablespoon of olive oil. When the oil is hot, put in the scallions, ginger, and chili bean sauce, and stir-fry for 1 minute. Add the stock, vinegar, chopped tomatoes, tomato purée, and soy sauce, and cook for a further minute. Set the sauce aside.

Pour 2–3 inches of oil into a medium saucepan and place over medium to high heat. The oil is ready when a cube of bread browns immediately. Dip the eggplant slices in the batter and deep-fry them in several batches, turning them until they are golden all over. Remove the slices with a slotted spoon and drain them on paper towels. Keep them warm in a moderate oven while cooking the rest. Arrange the eggplant on a warm plate, and serve hot, with the sauce in a small dish to pass around separately.

Savory Puff Pastry Rolls ~ *UK*

Preparation time:
15 minutes

Cooking time:
50 minutes

These rolls are great as a starter, snack, or cut smaller for a buffet. Kids love them, so why not make plenty, freeze them, and bake them straight from frozen.

SERVES 4 (MAKES APPROXIMATELY 15 ROLLS)

2 tablespoons olive oil
3 medium onions, chopped
4 vegetarian burgers (1/2 pound), broken into pieces
2/3 cup chopped mixed nuts
2 tablespoons tomato purée
1 tablespoon each freshly chopped sage and basil
sea salt and black pepper to taste
1/2 pound puff pastry
1 organic egg yolk or a little dairy or soy milk to glaze

Heat the oil in a medium saucepan, add the onions, and cover the pan. Soften the onions over gentle heat for about 15 minutes, stirring occasionally, until they are translucent. Add the burger pieces and cook for a further 3–4 minutes. Remove the burger and onions from the pan and put them into a bowl with the nuts, tomato purée, herbs, salt and pepper. Mix the ingredients thoroughly and allow the mixture to cool.

Roll the puff pastry into a rectangle 15 x 12 inches and cut it into three strips, each 5 inches wide. Form a third of the filling into a sausage along the center of each strip, leaving a 1-inch border on each side. Brush the top border with water and fold over the bottom border so it covers the filling. Fold the top border over the bottom and secure the edges by pressing them in firmly.

Cut the pastry rolls into five even lengths and transfer them to a baking sheet with the join underneath. Using a sharp knife, make three shallow cuts on the top of each one, brush with beaten egg yolk or a little milk, and bake at 400°F for about 25 minutes or until the rolls have risen and turned golden brown.

SPARE EGG WHITES

Leftover egg whites can be frozen easily in small containers. They must be thoroughly defrosted in the fridge before you use them.

Asparagus Crêpes with Tarragon and Crème Fraîche ~ *France*

Preparation time: 30 minutes (plus 2 hours resting time)

These elegant crêpes make a delicate starter for a special meal, and look very beautiful on the plate.

SERVES 6

BATTER

1¼ cups all-purpose flour, sifted
2 large organic eggs
1¼ cups dairy or soy milk
⅔ cup water
1 teaspoon vegetable oil, plus extra oil for frying
pinch of sea salt

FILLING

36 small, fresh asparagus spears, trimmed
2–3 tablespoons freshly chopped tarragon
1 cup crème fraîche or sour cream
1 teaspoon freshly squeezed lemon juice
1 teaspoon superfine sugar
black pepper to taste

For the batter, put the flour, eggs, milk, water, oil, and salt into a blender, and run it for 1 minute. Alternatively, sift the flour into a mediumbowl, add the eggs, and slowly whisk in the milk, water, oil, and salt to make a smooth batter. Let it rest for 2 hours.

Heat a 7-inch frying pan until hot, then moisten it with a small amount of oil. Carefully pour in 2 tablespoons of the batter and swirl it around the base of the pan to form a thin pancake. Cook the crêpe until it is golden and crisp on both sides. Remove it from the pan and keep it warm in a moderate oven between sheets of aluminum foil or wax paper while you make the other crêpes. Repeat the steps until you have made twelve crêpes in all. Brush the pan lightly with a little more oil if necessary between crêpes, and regulate the temperature of the pan to prevent them from burning.

Cook the asparagus until tender, standing it in boiling water so that the tips steam above the surface and the base of the asparagus is soft. This will take about 6–7 minutes. Drain the asparagus thoroughly; allow it to cool slightly before laying three spears in the middle of each crêpe.

Mix the chopped tarragon into the crème fraîche or sour cream and season to taste with the lemon juice, sugar, and pepper.

Spoon a little of the sauce over the warm asparagus, fold both sides of the crêpe over the center so that the asparagus protrudes at each end, and serve at once with the remaining sauce on the side.

TIP

When asparagus is out of season, you can replace it with 1 pound of leeks, washed, trimmed, and sliced across. The leeks will take longer to boil and need to be drained thoroughly, but leek crêpes make an equally splendid starter.

Asparagus Crêpes with Tarragon and Crème Fraîche

Broccoli and Parmesan Tartlets ~ *France*

A classic French starter, these individual tartlets also make a super light lunch. Serve them with Fennel and Arugula Salad (page 50).

Preparation time: **30 minutes**

Cooking time: **25–30 minutes**

SERVES 6

¾ pound Easy Shortcrust Pastry (page 153), or Crunchy Wholemeal Pastry (page 154)
½ large red onion, chopped finely
1 pound broccoli, steamed and cut into small florets
½ cup grated vegetarian Parmesan
4 large organic eggs
½ cup crème fraîche or soy cream
1 teaspoon ground cumin
black pepper to taste

Roll out the pastry thinly. Butter six 4-inch fluted tart pans with removable bases, and line them with the pastry. Bake them blind (page 161) and allow them to cool.

Scatter the chopped red onion on top of the pastry. Fill the tart shells with the broccoli and scatter half of the Parmesan on top.

Beat the eggs with the crème fraîche or soy cream and season with cumin and pepper. Pour the egg mixture over the broccoli. Sprinkle the top with the rest of the Parmesan.

Bake at 375°F for 25–30 minutes or until the pastry is crisp and the mixture has set in the center. Cool on a rack for 5 minutes, then remove the tartlets from the pans.

PARMESAN
Parmesan cheese is traditionally made using animal rennet. However, there are now a few brands of Parmesan available with vegetable agents. If you can't find one, substitute any finely grated mature vegetarian hard cheese.

Avocado Hummus V *Lebanon*

If, like me, you love traditional hummus, try this variation for a change. It is particularly good in a sandwich with chopped tomatoes, peppers, and red onion.

Preparation time: **10 minutes**

SERVES 6–8

1 cup canned chickpeas (garbanzo beans), drained
1 tablespoon tahini (sesame paste)
juice of 1 lemon
4 tablespoons plain dairy or soy yogurt
3 tablespoons olive oil
1 clove garlic, crushed
2 large ripe avocados, peeled and stoned
sea salt and black pepper to taste
freshly chopped parsley to garnish

Place the chickpeas in a blender with the main ingredients up to and including the avocados. Blend until well mixed and smooth. Season to taste with salt and pepper, adding more lemon juice if necessary.

Put the hummus into a serving bowl, cover, and chill in the fridge. Sprinkle with finely chopped parsley just before serving.

TIP
Add a couple of chopped fresh spinach leaves to enhance the color.

Caponata (Eggplant and Olive Sauce) V *Italy*

Preparation time:
1 hour

This classic Sicilian dish is delicious hot or cold, and is often enjoyed with grissini (bread sticks) or toasted bread as part of an antipasto. It sets off grilled vegetables beautifully and makes a delicious topping for pasta, pizza, or grilled polenta slices.

SERVES 4–6

10 tablespoons olive oil
1 large red onion, finely chopped
1 teaspoon tomato purée
2 tablespoons balsamic vinegar
1–2 tablespoons sugar
14-ounce can tomatoes with their juices, chopped
1 cup green olives, chopped
2 tablespoons capers, finely chopped
2 medium eggplants, finely chopped
sea salt and black pepper to taste

Heat 2 tablespoons of the oil in a large pan, add the onion and cook for 10 minutes over medium heat, until soft. Add the tomato purée and cook for 1 minute, add the vinegar, sugar, tomatoes, olives, and capers. Cook over medium heat for 20 minutes.

In a medium frying pan, fry the eggplant in two batches, using 4 tablespoons of oil for each batch, tossing and turning them for about 10 minutes until they are soft and lightly colored. Add the first batch to the tomato mixture before cooking the second.

Finally, mix everything together well, season to taste with salt and pepper, then allow the caponata to cool in a bowl. Check the seasoning again when it is cold, because the flavors mellow.

Pinto Bean Dip V *Mexico*

Preparation time:
10 minutes

When I visited the American Southwest, I had my first taste of Mexican food and it soon became one of my favorites. Now the whole family loves it and it's a real winner. It is packed with protein, as beans and corn feature predominately in most dishes.

SERVES 4–6

1¾ cups canned pinto beans, drained
1 tablespoon olive oil, plus a little extra
juice of 1 lemon or 2 limes
1 medium red onion, chopped
1 tablespoon coriander (or flat leaf parsley if preferred)
1 clove garlic
½ each green and red chili pepper, seeded and chopped, to garnish

Blend all the ingredients until smooth. Put the dip into a serving dish, sprinkle it with the chopped chili peppers, and drizzle a little olive oil over the top. Serve with tortilla chips or fresh vegetable sticks.

Chili Corn Fritters ~ *Thailand*

These crisp, golden corn fritters, spiked with chili and coriander, clearly show why Thai cuisine has become so popular in the West in recent years: they are irresistibly mouth-watering.

Preparation time: ***10 minutes***

Cooking time: ***25 minutes***

SERVES 3–4 (MAKES APPROXIMATELY 20 FRITTERS)

1 pound frozen or canned corn kernels, defrosted (if appropriate) and drained
1 cup all-purpose flour, sifted
2 teaspoons chili powder
1/4 teaspoon coriander seeds, crushed
1/4 teaspoon black pepper
2 tablespoons freshly chopped coriander (or flat leaf parsley if preferred)
1 small clove garlic, chopped
1/2-inch fresh ginger, chopped
pinch of sea salt
1–2 teaspoons soy sauce to taste
1 large or 2 small organic eggs, beaten
vegetable oil for shallow frying
Garlic Dipping Sauce (page 147)

Combine the corn with the other ingredients (except for the oil) in a medium bowl and mix well. Pour 1/4 inch of vegetable oil into a large frying pan and heat it until a little of the batter dropped into the oil sizzles immediately. Place 1 tablespoon of the batter at a time into the oil. Keep the fritters apart in the pan and fry until they are golden brown on both sides, about 4–5 minutes for each side. Repeat until all the batter has been used.

Drain the fritters on paper towels and keep them warm in a moderate oven until you have cooked them all and are ready to serve.

TIP
Instead of using chili powder in the fritters, use 1–2 fresh seeded and chopped red or green chili peppers with a pinch of cumin seeds, or 1 teaspoon red chili flakes, and a pinch of cumin seeds.

Melizanasalata (Eggplant Dip) V *Greece*

This keeps for days, covered, in the fridge. Serve it at room temperature, drizzled with a little olive oil and garnished with chopped parsley and black olives. Serve with warm pita bread.

Preparation time: ***1 hour***

SERVES 4–6

1 pound eggplant
1 small red onion, sliced finely
1 large clove garlic, crushed
1/4 cup olive oil
juice of 1/2 lemon
sea salt and black pepper to taste
freshly chopped parsley and a few halved olives to garnish (see above)

Prick the eggplant with a fork and bake it at 350°F for 40–45 minutes, turning once or twice. Let it cool, then peel it and chop the flesh, allowing the juices to run off.

Put the flesh into a blender with the onion, garlic, olive oil, lemon, salt and pepper, and blend well. Put the dip into a bowl and chill it in the fridge.

Chili Corn Fritters with Garlic Dipping Sauce

Fried Zucchini and Eggplant (V) *Greece*

Preparation time: 25 minutes

Arrange the zucchini and eggplant on a plate and place it in the center of the table, where everyone can help themselves. It is best served immediately.

SERVES 4

2 medium zucchini, washed and cut in quarters lengthwise and halved crosswise
1 large eggplant, trimmed and sliced into ½-inch circles
vegetable oil for shallow frying
sea salt and black pepper to taste
lemon quarters to garnish
Skorthalia Sauce (page 147)

TIP
Use the freshest zucchini with unblemished skin. It will turn slightly bitter if it is not used within a few days of purchase. Likewise, the eggplant needs to be fresh, with a smooth, deep purple skin.

Sift the flour onto a large plate and roll the prepared zucchini and eggplant in it until they are well coated.

Heat ¼ inch of oil in a large frying pan until it is hot. Add the zucchini sections and cook until they are golden brown, turning occasionally—they will take about 8 minutes, and will need to be cooked in batches. Remove them with a slotted spoon and drain them on paper towels. Keep them warm in a moderate oven.

Using fresh oil, fry the eggplant slices a few at a time until they are golden brown on both sides, removing and draining them as before. Keep them warm, and repeat until all the slices have been cooked.

Arrange the fried zucchini and eggplant on a warm plate and sprinkle them with salt and pepper to taste. Place lemon wedges around the edge of the plate, and serve with the Greek thick garlic sauce called skorthalia.

Fried Zucchini and Eggplant with Skorthalia Sauce

Curried Corn V *India*

An unusual way of serving corn, this dish makes the most of classic Indian flavors. Serve it with a traditional Indian bread such as naan or chapati.

Preparation time:
35 minutes

SERVES 4

4 tablespoons vegetable oil
2 cups frozen or canned corn, or kernels freshly cut from the cob
1 large onion, chopped finely
4 tablespoons freshly chopped coriander (or flat leaf parsley if preferred)
2 cloves garlic, crushed
1-inch fresh ginger, peeled and grated
2 teaspoons ground cumin
2 teaspoons curry powder
⅔ cup plain dairy or soy yogurt

Heat the oil in a large frying pan or wok and fry the corn for about 3 minutes over medium heat, turning until the kernels are lightly browned. Using a slotted spoon, remove the corn from the pan.

Add the onion to the pan and fry until it is soft, about 10 minutes, then add the coriander or parsley, garlic, and ginger. Stir well for 2 minutes, then add the spices. Simmer for 8–10 minutes, remove from the heat, and stir in the yogurt just before serving.

TIP
When corn is in season, use fresh kernels cut from the cob. To do this, hold the cob vertical and run a sharp knife down behind the kernels to remove them from the cob. Cut in strips until all the kernels have been removed.

Chile Con Queso V *Mexico*

Vegetarian burger can be used straight from the freezer. If you defrost it first, remember to adjust the cooking time accordingly.

Preparation time:
40 minutes

SERVES 6–8

2 tablespoons olive oil
1 red onion, chopped finely
¾ pound frozen vegetarian burger
4 anaheim or jalapeño chili peppers, seeded and chopped (page 123)
3 medium canned plum tomatoes, drained and chopped
⅔ cup light dairy or warmed soy cream
1 pound low-fat vegetarian cream cheese or soft soy "cheese"
sea salt to taste
freshly chopped coriander (or flat leaf parsley if preferred) to garnish

Heat the oil in a large frying pan, add the onion, and cover the pan. Soften the onion over low heat for about 10 minutes, stirring occasionally. Break the burger into pieces, add it to the pan, and cook, stirring, for 5 minute. Add the chilies and tomatoes, and simmer uncovered for about 10 minutes.

Mix the cream into the cream cheese and beat until smooth. Add this to the pan and stir over medium heat until hot. Season to taste with salt. Allow the chili to cool slightly before serving.

Garnish with chopped coriander or parsley, and serve with warm tortilla pieces or tortilla chips on the side.

Felafels ♥ *Lebanon*

Preparation time:
30 minutes
(plus chilling time)

Egyptian in origin, these West Lebanese felafels take some beating. Try serving them in pita bread with a combination of chopped scallion, tomato, radish, cucumber, lettuce, white cabbage, and pickled chili, dressed with Yogurt with Fresh Mint or Tahini Citrus Sauce (page 147).

SERVES 4 (MAKES APPROXIMATELY 20 FELAFELS)

3½ cups canned chickpeas (garbanzo beans), drained
1 teaspoon each ground cumin, turmeric, and sea salt
1 clove garlic, crushed
1 cup fresh breadcrumbs
3 tablespoons freshly chopped coriander (or flat leaf parsley if preferred)
2 tablespoons water
all-purpose flour to coat
vegetable oil for deep frying
sauce to serve (see above)

Put the chickpeas, spices, garlic, breadcrumbs, and preferred herb into a food processor. Process until the chickpeas are finely chopped but not puréed. Put the mixture into a large bowl and add the water. Knead the mixture and then, with floured hands, shape it into twenty walnut-size balls, slightly flattening each one. Chill them in the fridge for at least 30 minutes.

Pour 2–3 inches of oil into a medium saucepan and place over medium to high heat. The oil is ready when a cube of bread browns immediately. Roll the felafels in flour and deep-fry them in several batches until they are browned all over, about 2–3 minutes on each side, turning once. Drain on paper towels before serving.

Black-eyed Bean Cakes ~ *Africa*

Preparation time:
30 minutes

These fabulous bean cakes used to be cooked in markets throughout Africa centuries ago, but are almost a thing of the past—so now is the time to revive them!

SERVES 3–4 (MAKES 12 BEAN CAKES)

1¾ cups canned black-eyed peas, drained
1 medium onion, chopped finely
1 tablespoon freshly chopped coriander (or flat leaf parsley if preferred)
½ teaspoon each ground allspice, cumin, and cayenne
2 tablespoons breadcrumbs
2 large organic egg yolks
sea salt and black pepper to taste
2 tablespoons each all-purpose flour and sesame seeds
vegetable oil for shallow frying
Chunky Tomato Sauce with Harissa (page 146)

Combine the black-eyed peas, onion, coriander or parsley, spices, breadcrumbs, and egg yolks in a blender until smooth. Season with salt and pepper.

Roll tablespoons of the mixture in flour and coat them with sesame seeds. Heat ¼ inch of oil in a large frying pan until it is hot. Fry the bean cakes for 3–4 minutes on each side, until they are well browned. Drain on paper towels and serve them warm with the chunky tomato sauce.

Spring Rolls V *Vietnam*

These Vietnamese-style spring rolls are an interesting variation of the more commonly known Chinese spring roll. Serve them with Ginger Dipping Sauce.

Preparation time:
35 minutes

Cooking time:
35 minutes

SERVES 4–6 (MAKES APPROXIMATELY 20–24 SMALL SPRING ROLLS)

1/4 cup bean thread noodles, soaked in warm water for 5 minutes
1/3 cup carrots, grated finely
1/3 cup snow peas, sliced finely
3 tablespoons finely sliced scallions
2 teaspoons dark sesame oil
1 teaspoon rice wine vinegar
2 tablespoons soy sauce
paprika to taste
1 package rice papers, or spring roll wrappers (or filo pastry cut into 5 x 5-inch squares)
peanut oil for deep frying
sprigs of mint, washed and dried
small crisp lettuce leaves to garnish, washed and dried
Ginger Dipping Sauce (page 146)

Drain the noodles and chop them roughly into 3-inch lengths. In a medium bowl, mix the noodles with the carrots, snow peas, scallions, sesame oil, vinegar, and soy sauce. Season to taste with paprika.

If you are using rice papers, fill a large bowl with warm water and dip them into it one at a time to soften. Dry them on a clean tea towel, and put 1 tablespoon of the filling in the middle of the paper. Fold in each side, then roll it up tightly. Repeat until you have used up all the filling.

Pour 2–3 inches of oil into a medium saucepan and place over medium to high heat. The oil is ready when a cube of bread browns immediately. Deep-fry the spring rolls a few at a time until they are golden brown all over. Drain them on paper towels and allow them to cool slightly.

TIP

When serving, place a dish of crisp lettuce leaves and sprigs of fresh mint on the table. Before eating each roll, place a small mint leaf onto a lettuce leaf and wrap this around the spring roll.

SOUPS

Vegetable Stock V

Homemade stock is the best, but if you are in a hurry a vegetable stock cube is a good option.

Preparation time:
25 minutes

MAKES 3 QUARTS

1 leek
2 onions
3 carrots
4 celery stalks
5 cloves garlic
6 peppercorns
1 bay leaf, a few parsley stalks and a few sprigs of thyme
7 cups water
sea salt to taste

Peel and clean all the vegetables, and chop them coarsely. Put them into a large saucepan with the rest of the ingredients and bring to a boil. Reduce the heat and simmer for 20 minutes. Remove the pan from the heat and leave the stock to cool completely. Strain and chill it in the fridge.

TIP
Use up cooking water left from steaming vegetables both in stock and in gravy (page 149) for extra flavor.

Plantain and Corn Soup V *Africa*

Plantains are a kind of cooking banana, which is firmer and starchier than regular bananas. They are best cooked and eaten as a vegetable. If you can't find plantains, squash or pumpkin also work well.

Preparation time:
25 minutes

SERVES 4

2 tablespoons vegetable oil
1 onion, chopped finely
1 clove garlic, crushed
1 pound yellow (half-ripe) plantains, peeled and sliced
1 large tomato, skinned and chopped
¾ cup corn kernels (fresh or frozen)
1 teaspoon dried or 2 teaspoons freshly chopped tarragon
5 cups vegetable stock (see above)
1 green chili pepper, seeded and chopped finely
pinch of grated nutmeg
sea salt and black pepper to taste
4 sprigs of fresh tarragon to garnish

Heat the oil in a large saucepan and add the onion and garlic. Fry for 5–6 minutes over medium heat until the onion is soft.

Add the plantains, tomato, and corn, and cook for 5 minutes, stirring.

Add the tarragon, stock, chili pepper, nutmeg, salt and pepper. Simmer for 10–15 minutes or until the plantain is tender.

Serve in individual bowls, garnished with a sprig of fresh tarragon.

TIP
Plantains are not that easy to peel. For slices, cut the plantain across at intervals and soak the pieces in salted water for about 30 minutes or until you can ease the pieces out of the skin. Keep them in the water until you need them to prevent them from discoloring. For strips, cut down the length of the plantain, not too deeply but just enough so that you can use a small knife to help pry off the skin.

Tom Yum Soup v *Thailand*

Preparation time:
30 minutes

This light soup demonstrates the characteristic flavors of Thai cooking—lemon grass, chili, and coconut.

SERVES 6

4 cups vegetable stock (page 32)
1¾ cups canned coconut milk
3 tablespoons freshly chopped coriander (optional)
2 tablespoons peanut oil
2 tablespoons finely chopped garlic
1 medium onion, chopped finely
1 fresh chili pepper, seeded and chopped finely
2 stalks lemon grass
¾ pound eggplant, cut into ½-inch cubes
1 cup canned chopped tomatoes
2 teaspoons sugar
sea salt and white pepper to taste
½ cup cooked basmati or Thai jasmine rice
6 tablespoons finely chopped roasted or raw peanuts to garnish

TIP
If you can't find canned coconut milk, you can make your own by pouring hot milk (or boiling water) over dried coconut in a bowl or jug, and allowing it to stand for 20 minutes before straining it.

In a medium saucepan, bring the stock and coconut milk to a simmer. For a more Asian flavor, add a small handful of fresh coriander to the stock.

Heat a wok or large frying pan and add the oil. When it is hot, add the garlic, onion, chili pepper, and lemon grass, and stir-fry over high heat for 2 minutes, then add the eggplant and cook for about 4 minutes until it has browned. Stir in the tomatoes and sugar, and mix well.

Add the vegetables to the stock, season to taste with salt and pepper, and simmer for about 5 minutes. Add the rice 2 minutes before the end of the cooking time.

Remove the lemon grass, and pour the soup into individual bowls. Garnish with chopped peanuts.

Cucumber, Quark, and Dill Soup ~ *Germany*

Preparation time:
10 minutes
(plus chilling time)

This soup is simple to make and brings out the light summery flavors of cucumber and fresh dill. Quark is a German low-fat soft cheese made from skim milk, and is high in protein. A good low-calorie alternative to cream cheese, it can be eaten on its own or used as an ingredient for cooking.

SERVES 4

1¾ cups quark, or low-fat cream cheese
3 tablespoons lemon juice
2 tablespoons freshly chopped dill
2½ cups vegetable stock (page 32)
1 large cucumber, peeled and coarsely grated
sea salt and black pepper to taste
4 sprigs of fresh dill to garnish

In a large bowl, mash together the quark, lemon juice, dill, and stock, and stir until smooth. Mix in the grated cucumber.

Chill the soup in the fridge for a minimum of 1 hour, then season with salt and pepper to taste and serve garnished with dill.

Hot and Sour Soup V *China*

You'll find variations of this soup all over East Asia, where the philosophy of cooking focuses on health and well-being.

Preparation time:
1 hour 10 minutes

SERVES 4

2 tablespoons cornstarch blended with 5 tablespoons water
4 tablespoons rice or white wine vinegar
3 tablespoons water
1 tablespoon dry sherry
2 tablespoons light soy sauce
black pepper to taste
2 tablespoons vegetable oil
3 slices fresh ginger, shredded finely
1 medium onion, sliced finely
3/4 cup shiitake mushrooms, shredded
2 cups water
1 tablespoon Chinese or porcini dried mushrooms, soaked in hot water for 20 minutes, then drained and sliced
1 1/2 cups canned straw mushrooms, halved
3-ounce can bamboo shoots, cut into matchsticks
2 scallions, shredded
1 green or red chili pepper, sliced lengthwise and seeded
2 1/2 cups vegetable stock (see tip below)
1/2 cup frozen peas, defrosted
chopped scallions to garnish

Mix the cornstarch, vinegar, water, sherry, and soy sauce together until smooth. Season to taste with pepper.

Heat the oil in a wok or large frying pan over medium heat and stir-fry the ginger, onion, and shiitake mushrooms for 2 minutes. Add the water, bring it to a boil and add the dried mushrooms, straw mushrooms, bamboo shoots, scallions, chili pepper, and stock.

Bring to a boil and simmer gently for 30 minutes, then add the peas and heat them through. Cook gently for 3 minutes, then slowly stir in the vinegar mixture until the soup thickens.

Remove the chili pepper and garnish with chopped scallions before serving.

TIP
Save the water from the dried mushrooms to use for the stock and top it up with vegetable stock (page 32).

Broccoli and Stilton Soup ~ *UK*

Stilton is unique to three specific counties in the East Midlands of England—Leicestershire, Nottinghamshire, and Derbyshire—and the traditional recipe can't officially be made anywhere else in the world.

Preparation time: ***35 minutes***

SERVES 4–6

4 tablespoons (1/2 stick) butter or margarine
1 small red onion, chopped
1 pound broccoli, chopped roughly
3 tablespoons wholemeal flour
5 cups vegetable stock (page 32)
5–6 spinach leaves, washed (optional)
3 tablespoons vegetarian Stilton cheese, crumbled
black pepper to taste
pinch of chili powder (optional)

Heat the butter or margarine in a large saucepan, add the onion, cover, and cook over medium heat. Soften the onion for 5 minutes, stirring occasionally. Add the broccoli and toss it with the onion for a further 5 minutes until it is tender.

Sprinkle the flour over the broccoli and toss again until it is thoroughly incorporated. Add the stock, stirring all the time. Bring the soup to simmering point and cook gently, covered, for 10 minutes or until the broccoli is completely soft. Stir in the spinach leaves for the last 2 minutes to enhance the color, if you wish.

Remove the pan from the heat, purée the soup in a blender, and put it back in the pan. Return the pan to the heat and stir in the crumbled cheese until it melts. Season to taste with pepper and a little chili powder.

GARNISHES FOR SOUP

An attractive and well thought out garnish can make all the difference to a soup. Fresh herbs are a popular choice and they should be chosen to enhance or lift the flavor of the soup. Other effective garnishes are grated or crumbled cheese, vegetarian bacon bits, toasted nuts, croûtons, chopped scallion, or diced cucumber. Always add your chosen garnish at the last moment. I like to add a swirl of soy cream, crème fraîche, or olive oil, as it always adds an attractive finishing touch.

Green Jade Soup V *China*

Preparation time:
20 minutes

A delicate soup from China, this is a simple combination of spinach and corn lightly flavored with soy sauce.

SERVES 4–6

½ pound cooked or frozen leaf spinach, thawed (1 pound fresh)
7-ounce can corn, drained and blended roughly
2 teaspoons cornstarch
2 tablespoons water
4 cups vegetable stock (page 32)
2 tablespoons soy sauce
black pepper to taste
4 scallions, white part only

TIP
Cut a deep cross into the leaf end of the scallions and let them soak in cold or ice water in the fridge until they open like flowers.

Put the spinach and corn into a large saucepan and heat them to a simmer for about 4–5 minutes. Mix the cornstarch with the water and stir it into the pan to thicken the juices released by the vegetables.

Gradually add the stock, stirring all the time. Add the soy sauce and mix it in well, then season to taste with pepper. Simmer the soup for 2 minutes.

Serve at once, garnishing each portion with a scallion flower (see tip).

French Onion Soup V *France*

Preparation time:
1 hour

This soup was made famous at Les Halles when it was the market area in Paris.

SERVES 6

4 tablespoons vegetable oil
2¼ pounds white onions, sliced thinly
1 teaspoon sugar
7½ cups vegetable stock (page 32)
⅔ cup dry red wine
sea salt and black pepper to taste
12 slices French bread
3 cloves garlic, halved
½ pound vegetarian Gruyère, grated (omit for vegans)

In a large, heavy saucepan, heat the oil and add the onions. Cook gently, stirring, over medium heat until they are covered with oil, then reduce the heat and cover the pan. Cook for 30 minutes until the onions are soft and brown, stirring occasionally.

Add the sugar and pour in the vegetable stock and wine. Simmer for 20 minutes and season to taste with salt and pepper.

Preheat the broiler. Just before the soup is ready, toast the slices of bread on both sides, then rub them with the cut cloves of garlic. Ladle the soup into six ovenproof bowls and put two slices of the toasted bread on top of each serving.

Sprinkle the grated cheese on the bread and place the bowls under the broiler until the cheese melts and bubbles and begins to brown. Serve at once.

Vegetable Soup with Coconut V *Africa*

A combination of turnip, sweet potato, and pumpkin, laced with silky coconut and fired by chili, this soup is as full of contrasts as the African continent itself.

Preparation time: 50–55 minutes

SERVES 4

2 tablespoons vegetable oil
1 large onion, chopped
1 cup each turnip, sweet potato, and pumpkin, peeled and cubed
1 teaspoon dried marjoram
1½ teaspoons each ground ginger and cinnamon
sea salt and black pepper to taste
1 tablespoon chopped scallion
5 cups vegetable stock (page 32)
2 tablespoons flaked almonds
1 chili pepper, seeded and chopped
1 teaspoon sugar
½ cup creamed coconut
freshly chopped coriander (or flat leaf parsley if preferred) to garnish

In a large saucepan, heat the oil, add the onion, and cook it gently for 4–5 minutes. Add the cubed vegetables and toss them over medium heat for a further 5–6 minutes.

Add the marjoram, ginger, cinnamon, salt, and pepper, and cook over low heat for 10 minutes, stirring frequently.

Add the scallion, stock, almonds, chili pepper, and sugar, and simmer gently for 10–15 minutes until the vegetables are just tender. Check the seasoning.

Grate the coconut into the soup and stir well. Sprinkle with chopped coriander or parsley and serve.

Scotch Broth V *Scotland*

In Scotland this hearty soup is sometimes referred to as "barley broth." The leek and root vegetables are traditional ingredients.

Preparation time: 1 hour 30 minutes

SERVES 6–8

3¾ quarts vegetable stock (page 32)
¾ cup pearl barley
2 medium carrots, peeled and sliced
1 white turnip or ½ cup rutabaga, peeled and diced
1 leek, cleaned and cut into thin slices
2 stalks celery, sliced thinly
1 large onion, chopped small
¾ cup Savoy or green cabbage, sliced into narrow ribbons
¾ cup frozen peas, defrosted
sea salt and black pepper to taste

In a stockpot, heat the stock and add the barley. Bring to a boil, cover, and simmer for 45 minutes.

Add the remaining ingredients to the pot (except for the peas) and bring it to a boil again. Simmer gently, covered, for 30 minutes or until the barley is cooked. Add the peas for the last 7–8 minutes.

Season to taste with salt and pepper, and serve in large soup bowls.

Vegetable Soup with Coconut

Spicy Lentil Soup with Sausages V *Germany*

This lentil soup is a complete meal in a bowl. It is lovely served with thick wedges of bread, or it can be made into a more substantial meal by serving it with Dumplings (page 152).

Preparation time: ***45 minutes***

SERVES 4–6

2 tablespoons olive oil
2 medium onions, chopped finely
2 large carrots, chopped
4 stalks celery, chopped finely
1 dried red chili pepper (optional)
2 cloves garlic, crushed
1 teaspoon ground coriander
1 teaspoon ground cumin
1 cup red lentils
6 cups vegetable stock (page 32)
⅔ cup tomato juice
8 vegetarian sausages, grilled
sea salt and black pepper to taste
freshly chopped parsley to garnish

Heat the oil in a large saucepan. Add the chopped onion, carrots, and celery, and optional chili pepper, and cook over low heat for 5 minutes, stirring occasionally.

Stir in the garlic and spices. Cook for a further minute or two, then stir in the lentils. Gradually stir in the stock and the tomato juice. Cover and simmer for about 20 minutes until the vegetables are tender.

Cut the grilled sausages into thick slices. Remove the soup from the heat and stir in the sausage slices. Season to taste with salt and pepper.

Serve sprinkled with chopped parsley.

Ravioli and Spinach Broth V *Italy*

The success of this soup relies on the vegetable stock, so use one with lots of rich flavor, such as that on page 32.

Preparation time: ***25 minutes***

SERVES 4

7½ cups vegetable stock
16 small or 8 large fresh ravioli filled with your favorite vegetarian filling
½ pound baby spinach leaves, washed
sea salt and black pepper to taste
2 tablespoons freshly chopped parsley to garnish
grated vegetarian Parmesan (optional)

In a large saucepan, heat the stock to simmering point and add the ravioli (check the cooking time given on the package). As soon as it floats to the top, stir in the spinach and simmer gently for a further 2 minutes.

Ladle the soup into bowls, season to taste with salt and pepper, and sprinkle parsley on top. Serve at once, with grated Parmesan to pass around (omit this for vegans).

Spicy Lentil Soup with Sausages

Chilled Red Pepper and Lime Soup ▼ *France*

This stunning soup is incredibly quick to make considering the sophisticated result.

Preparation time: 5 minutes

SERVES 4

8-ounce can or 2 medium red bell peppers, grilled and skinned
juice of 2 limes
2 tablespoons olive oil
14-ounce can chopped tomatoes with their juices
¼ cup crème fraîche or soy cream
1 teaspoon sugar
½ teaspoon cayenne pepper
ice water
crème fraîche or soy cream and freshly chopped rosemary to garnish
sea salt and black pepper to taste

Put the peppers into a blender with the lime juice, olive oil, and chopped tomatoes, and blend to a smooth purée. Stir in the crème fraîche or soy cream and add the sugar and cayenne. Mix well, then chill in the fridge for at least 2 hours.

Stir well and thin to a pouring consistency with ice water and season to taste with salt and pepper. Garnish each bowl with a swirl of crème fraîche or soy cream and a little freshly chopped rosemary before serving.

Black Bean Soup ▼ *Brazil*

Black beans (*frijoles negro*) are kidney-shaped beans native to South America and are traditionally used in stews and soups.

Preparation time: 1 hour 30 minutes (plus soaking time)

SERVES 4–6

½ cup black beans, soaked for a minimum of 8 hours
2 tablespoons vegetable oil
1 medium onion, chopped
2 cloves garlic, sliced
1–2 green chili peppers, seeded and chopped
5 cups vegetable stock (page 32)
2 tablespoons tomato purée
1 bay leaf
1¼ cups soy milk, warmed
4 tablespoons freshly chopped coriander (or flat leaf parsley if preferred) to garnish
sea salt and black pepper to taste

Drain and rinse the beans thoroughly. In a large saucepan, heat the oil over medium heat and cook the onion, garlic, and chili peppers, stirring occasionally until softened, for about 5 minutes.

Add the beans, stock, tomato purée, and bay leaf, and bring to a boil. Boil for 10 minutes, then reduce the heat, cover, and simmer for a further 50 minutes, or until the beans are tender.

Cook for at least 10–15 minutes, then remove the bay leaf and purée the mixture in a blender until smooth.

Return the soup to the saucepan, then stir in the soy milk and reheat it gently. Stir in the coriander or parsley before serving and season to taste with salt and pepper.

Chilled Red Pepper and Lime Soup

Pasta and Fava Bean Soup V *Italy*

Preparation time:
1 hour 30 minutes

This Italian mixture of pasta and fava beans makes a nourishing meal, served with warm Italian bread. If you don't have time to soak the beans, use canned ones instead—they are just as good, but remember to halve the cooking time.

SERVES 6–8

5 tablespoons olive oil
2 cloves garlic, chopped small
2 large carrots, peeled and diced
1 large onion, cubed
2 stalks celery, trimmed and diced small
14-ounce can chopped tomatoes
7 cups vegetable stock (page 32)
1 cup fava or cannellini beans, soaked for a minimum 8 hours
4 tablespoons freshly chopped parsley
1 tablespoon freshly chopped oregano, rosemary, or thyme
1 bay leaf
1¼ cups macaroni or any small pasta
sea salt and black pepper to taste

In a stockpot, heat the oil over medium heat, add the garlic, carrots, onion, and celery, and sauté for 5 minutes. Then add the chopped tomatoes, stock, beans, parsley, oregano or other herb, and the bay leaf. Bring to a boil, boil rapidly for 10 minutes, then reduce the heat, cover, and simmer for 40–50 minutes until the beans are just tender.

Add the pasta and cook for a further 10 minutes, so that it becomes soft and well cooked. Season to taste with salt and pepper.

Tomato and Rosemary Soup V *USA*

Cooking time:
10 minutes

Tomato soup has always been a family favorite. This recipe, with its hint of rosemary, is light, creamy, and refreshing, and especially good in the summer when tomatoes are at their best.

SERVES 4

3 tablespoons margarine, or 2½ tablespoons vegetable oil
1 tablespoon all-purpose flour
⅔ cup soy cream
⅔ cup soy milk
2 sprigs of rosemary
Tomato Coulis (page 150), warmed
sea salt and black pepper to taste

In a medium saucepan, melt the margarine or heat the oil over low heat and stir in the flour. Add the cream slowly, stirring all the time, until smooth. Then slowly stir in the milk and add a sprig of rosemary.

Stir in the tomato coulis slowly, so that the soup does not separate. Simmer very gently for 2 minutes.

Season to taste with salt and pepper, then serve garnished with rosemary.

Pasta and Fava Bean Soup

Minted Pea and Spinach Soup (V) *UK*

This soup is beautiful in color and flavor. It can be served, either hot or chilled, with croûtons.

Preparation time: 30 minutes

SERVES 4–6

2 tablespoons (1/4 stick) butter or margarine
1 large onion, chopped
1 pound fresh spinach leaves, washed
1 cup frozen peas, defrosted
4 cups vegetable stock (page 32)
3 tablespoons freshly chopped mint
2/3 cup crème fraîche, or warmed soy cream, plus extra to garnish
fresh mint leaves to garnish
Croûtons (page 152)

In a large saucepan, heat the butter or margarine over medium heat, add the onion, and cook until it softens, for about 5 minutes.

Shred the spinach, add it to the pan, and stir until it wilts. Add the peas and stir again. Gradually add half of the stock, stirring, and bring it to a boil. Simmer for 5 minutes, stirring occasionally.

Purée the soup in a blender. Return it to the pan, add the chopped mint, and stir for a further 2 minutes, then add the rest of the stock and heat it through.

Remove the pan from the heat, stir in the crème fraîche or soy cream, and reheat the soup gently. Serve garnished with fresh mint leaves and crème fraîche or soy cream.

Cream of Broccoli and Squash Soup (V) *USA*

A smooth, blended soup, this is wonderful food for cold weather. I sometimes use pumpkin instead of squash. Serve sprinkled with chopped chives.

Preparation time: 40–45 minutes

SERVES 6–8

4 tablespoons olive oil
1 medium onion, diced
2 medium cloves garlic, crushed
1 1/2 pounds broccoli, chopped
1 pound squash or pumpkin, peeled and chopped
1 large bay leaf
1 teaspoon sea salt
5 cups vegetable stock (page 32)
2 1/2 cups dairy or warmed soy cream
1/2 teaspoon each dried marjoram, thyme, and basil
black pepper to taste
freshly chopped chives to garnish

In a stockpot, heat the oil, add the onion and garlic, and cook over low heat until translucent, for about 10 minutes. Add the broccoli, squash or pumpkin, bay leaf, salt, and stock. Cover and simmer for 15–20 minutes until the vegetables are tender. Blend until smooth.

Return the soup to the pan and stir in the cream. Add the dried herbs and season to taste with pepper. Simmer gently for a further 10 minutes before serving.

Minted Pea and Spinach Soup with Croûtons

Watercress and Potato Soup V *France*

This is very simple to make and full of minerals and vitamins.

Preparation time:
30 minutes

SERVES 4

1 pound potatoes, peeled and chopped
1 medium onion, chopped
4 cups vegetable stock (page 32)
$1\frac{1}{4}$ cups skim dairy or warmed soy milk
2 bunches watercress, trimmed and chopped finely
large pinch of ground nutmeg
sea salt and black pepper to taste

In a large saucepan, simmer the potatoes and the onion in the stock until tender, for about 20 minutes. Blend to a smooth purée.

Stir in the milk and add the chopped watercress. Simmer for 2–3 minutes, then season to taste with nutmeg, salt, and pepper.

TIP
You can prepare the potato and onion base in advance and reheat it when you add the milk and watercress.

Green Minestrone V *Italy*

A great classic of Italian cuisine, minestrone never fails to be popular. This recipe, using all green vegetables with fresh summer herbs, is light and delicate.

Preparation time:
1 hour 30 minutes

SERVES 6

3 tablespoons olive oil
2 cloves garlic, crushed
4–5 scallions, chopped finely
4 stalks celery, sliced finely
$\frac{1}{2}$ pound broccoli, cut into florets
$\frac{1}{2}$ pound green beans, cut into short lengths
$\frac{3}{4}$ cup frozen peas
$\frac{1}{3}$ pound cabbage, shredded finely
medium bunch of fresh parsley, chopped finely
$2\frac{1}{2}$ quarts vegetable stock (page 32)
$1\frac{1}{2}$ cups very small pasta shapes
3–4 tablespoons mixed freshly chopped herbs (such as basil, oregano, marjoram, or thyme)
sea salt and black pepper to taste
freshly grated vegetarian Parmesan (optional)

In a large stockpot, heat the oil, add the garlic, scallions, and celery, and cook over medium heat for 5 minutes.

Add the rest of the vegetables and the parsley, and stir for 2 minutes. Gradually add the stock. Bring it to a boil and simmer, covered, for 30 minutes. Remove from the heat and stir in the pasta.

Let the soup sit, uncovered, for 15 minutes, until the pasta is soft, then stir in the chopped herbs and season to taste with salt and pepper.

Serve hot, with grated Parmesan (omit this for vegans).

TIP
Minestrone is even tastier the day after it is made, when the flavors have developed.

SALADS

Lettuce Hearts with Avocado, Croûtons, and Blue Cheese Dressing ~ *USA*

I discovered this wonderful salad while visiting the West Coast of America and enjoyed it so much that I decided to include it here. I often make it when friends come for lunch.

Preparation time:
15 minutes

SERVES 4

Croûtons (page 152), using 4 slices of wholegrain bread
3 tablespoons vegetarian blue cheese
Classic Vinaigrette (page 151)
2 tablespoons sour cream
black pepper to taste
3 lettuce hearts
2 medium ripe avocados, peeled and stoned
finely chopped chives to garnish

Prepare the croûtons.

Crumble the cheese and mix it thoroughly into the vinaigrette until smooth. Add the sour cream and season to taste with pepper.

Remove any bruised outer leaves of the lettuce. Cut the lettuce lengthwise into quarters, rinse them, and pat dry. Slice the avocados thinly. Put three segments of lettuce on each plate with some slices of avocado. Spoon the dressing over the top. Scatter with the croûtons and finish with pepper to taste and a sprinkling of chives.

Fennel and Arugula Salad V *Italy*

Lovely and simple, this salad is hard to beat. It is perfect for a light summer lunch.

Preparation time:
10 minutes

SERVES 6

3 large fennel bulbs
¾ pound arugula, washed and dried
¼ cup olive oil
1 tablespoon balsamic vinegar
sea salt and black pepper to taste
3 tablespoons vegetarian Parmesan, shaved finely, to garnish (optional)

Trim the fennel and remove the outside layer. Cut the bulbs into quarters and slice the quarters into thin crescents. Combine the fennel with the arugula in a salad bowl.

Mix the olive oil with the vinegar and season to taste with salt and pepper. Toss the salad with the dressing, check the seasoning, and lay the shaved Parmesan on top before serving (omit this for vegans).

TIP

You can buy a packet of seeds and grow arugula on your windowsill. It is easy to grow and far less expensive than buying it at the supermarket.

Lettuce Hearts with Avocado, Croûtons, and Blue Cheese Dressing

Crispy Rice Noodle and Tofu Salad V *China*

A salad as attractive as this one also makes a wonderful starter. The crispy noodles, firm tofu, and crunchy beansprouts are invigorated by the tangy dressing.

Preparation time: 25 minutes

SERVES 4

peanut oil for deep frying
½ cup rice noodles
¾ cup firm tofu, cut into ½-inch cubes
½ cup beansprouts
3 scallions, chopped finely
1 fresh chili pepper, seeded and chopped
4 tablespoons freshly chopped coriander (or flat leaf parsley if preferred)
1–2 cloves garlic, crushed, to taste
3 tablespoons yellow bean sauce
1 tablespoon sugar
3 tablespoons cider vinegar
4 sprigs of fresh coriander (or flat leaf parsley if preferred) to garnish

Heat 2–3 inches of oil in a medium saucepan and place over medium to high heat. The oil is ready when a cube of bread browns immediately. Deep-fry the noodles briefly, in several batches, until they puff up. Remove them with a slotted spoon and drain them well on paper towels.

Deep-fry the cubed tofu until golden, remove it with a slotted spoon, and drain it on paper towels.

Divide the crispy noodles among four individual bowls and garnish them with the tofu, beansprouts, scallions, chili pepper, and chopped coriander or parsley.

Mix the garlic, yellow bean sauce, sugar, and vinegar together. Pour the dressing over the salad just before serving, and garnish with coriander or parsley sprigs.

Cajun Rice Salad V *USA*

Peppers of every kind are crucial to Cajun cooking: this colorful salad uses red and yellow bell peppers, green chili peppers, and peppery spices. Make it as chili-hot as you can stand to give this vigorous dish its authentic Cajun effect!

Preparation time: 30 minutes

SERVES 4–6

⅔ cup long-grain rice
3 tablespoons each chopped red and yellow bell pepper
2 tablespoons canned mild green chili peppers, chopped finely
⅓ cup red onion, chopped finely
1–2 stalks celery, chopped finely
Creole Vinaigrette (page 151)
Tabasco to taste (optional)
4 scallions, chopped finely
small bunch of parsley, chopped finely

Cook the rice according to the instructions on the package. Combine the rice, peppers, red onion, and celery in a salad bowl. Toss thoroughly with sufficient vinaigrette to moisten the salad and season to taste with the optional Tabasco. Sprinkle with the chopped scallions and parsley before serving.

Crispy Rice Noodle and Tofu Salad

Louisiana Potato Salad ~ *USA*

A light spicing of Tabasco in this salad gives it its regional flavor, as Tabasco Pepper Sauce was originally created by the McIlhenny family of Louisiana in the 1860s.

Preparation time: **20 minutes (plus 1 hour marinating)**

Cooking time: **20 minutes**

SERVES 6

10 medium waxy potatoes, unpeeled
Classic Vinaigrette (page 151)
2 tablespoons each red and green bell pepper, chopped finely
1 large celery stalk, chopped finely
1 small red onion, chopped finely
sea salt and black pepper to taste
Tabasco to taste
3–4 scallions, chopped finely
½ cup finely chopped parsley

Quarter the potatoes and put them in a large saucepan, cover with boiling water, and cook until they are tender. Drain, allow them to cool slightly, and cut them into slices ½ inch thick. Put them in a large bowl and toss with sufficient vinaigrette to moisten them, and allow them to marinate for at least 1 hour. Then mix in the chopped vegetables and season to taste with salt, pepper, and Tabasco.

When you are ready to serve, garnish the salad with the scallions and parsley.

Watercress Salad with Mushrooms and Gruyère ~ *Switzerland*

Gruyère is an excellent choice for this salad, as its firm texture and sweet, nutty flavor combine so well with the other ingredients.

Preparation time: **10 minutes**

SERVES 4

2 bunches of watercress, washed and trimmed
1 cup mushrooms, sliced thinly
1 tablespoon freshly chopped thyme
1 cup vegetarian Gruyère cheese, grated
1 clove garlic, crushed
Classic Vinaigrette (page 151)
sea salt and black pepper to taste

Combine the watercress, mushrooms, and thyme in a large salad bowl, and toss with the grated cheese.

Mix the garlic into the vinaigrette and season to taste with salt and pepper. Toss the salad with sufficient vinaigrette and serve immediately.

Cephalonian Salad ~ *Greece*

Preparation time: 15 minutes

This salad originates from the Greek island of Cephalonia. The addition of dill sets off the more traditional ingredients beautifully and the lemon dressing gives it a real zing.

SERVES 4

1 medium Romaine lettuce
4 tablespoons freshly chopped dill or fennel
5–6 scallions, shredded finely
1 green bell pepper, seeded and cut into thin strips
3 large ripe tomatoes, chopped
12–15 black olives, pitted
¼ pound vegetarian feta cheese, cubed
4 tablespoons extra virgin olive oil
2 tablespoons lemon juice
sea salt and black pepper to taste

TIP
To enhance the flavor of the tomatoes, sprinkle them with a little sea salt and let them marinate for a few minutes.

Discard any bruised outer leaves of the lettuce and shred the rest very finely by rolling them into cigar shapes and cutting them as thinly as possible. In a large bowl, mix the lettuce with the dill or fennel and the scallions. Toss in the green pepper, tomatoes, olives, and feta.

Mix the oil and lemon juice, and season to taste with salt and pepper. Carefully fold the dressing into the salad just before serving.

Baby Spinach and Avocado with Mushrooms and "Bacon" Ⓥ *USA*

Preparation time: 25–30 minutes

This salad combination has become something of a modern classic, and this version using vegetarian bacon is even better than the original.

SERVES 4

1 large ripe avocado, peeled and stoned
6–8 scallions, sliced finely
1 cup firm button mushrooms, sliced thinly
½ pound baby spinach leaves, washed and torn into medium strips
Classic Vinaigrette (page 151)
4 tablespoons vegetarian bacon bits, or 4 vegetarian bacon strips, fried and chopped

Slice the avocado and put it in a large bowl with the scallions, sliced mushrooms, and spinach. Add sufficient vinaigrette and toss lightly. Sprinkle with the bacon pieces and serve immediately.

Artichoke, Goat's Cheese, and Walnut Salad ~ *France*

Preparation time: 15 minutes

This salad is from the Perigord region in southwestern France, which is famous for its walnuts. The subtle flavor of the oil enhances the other flavors of this salad wonderfully.

SERVES 4

½ cup green beans, trimmed
½ butterhead or Boston lettuce
bunch of watercress
14-ounce can artichoke hearts, sliced (approximately 5)
¼ pound vegetarian goat's cheese, crumbled or diced
⅓ cup walnuts, toasted (page 70) and chopped small
3 tablespoons walnut oil, or olive oil
1 tablespoon tarragon vinegar
1 clove garlic, crushed
sea salt and black pepper to taste

Steam the beans lightly for 5–6 minutes until they are cooked but still slightly crisp. Plunge them into cold water to cool, and cut them into 2-inch lengths.

Tear the lettuce into strips, break the watercress into short lengths, and put them in a large bowl with the artichokes, cheese, and walnuts.

Make the dressing with the oil, vinegar, and garlic, and season to taste with salt and pepper. Pour it over the salad, toss lightly, and serve at once.

Surfers' Salad V *USA*

Preparation time: 15–20 minutes

My son James created this energizing salad on a surfing holiday. You could experiment with different flavored oils in your vinaigrette (page 80).

SERVES 4

1 soft lettuce, such as Boston, washed and dried
¼ cup baby spinach leaves, washed and dried
1 bunch of watercress and/or lambs' lettuce, washed and dried
½ cup beansprouts
¼ pound carrots, peeled and grated or sliced finely
3 tablespoons alfalfa sprouts
handful of basil leaves, torn roughly
4 large scallions, halved and sliced lengthwise
Classic Vinaigrette (page 151)

Combine the ingredients in a large salad bowl. Toss with sufficient vinaigrette, and serve immediately.

Artichoke, Goat's Cheese, and Walnut Salad

Cannellini Bean Salad ▼ *Greece*

Bean salads are characteristic of Greek home cooking. This one is deliciously spiked with lemon and onion, and garnished with black olives and fresh oregano.

Preparation time:
10 minutes

SERVES 2–4

4 tablespoons olive oil
juice of ½ lemon
sea salt and black pepper to taste
2 cups canned cannellini (white kidney) or haricot (navy) beans, drained
1 small red onion, sliced finely
3 tablespoons freshly chopped parsley
12–16 black olives, pitted
2 hard-boiled eggs, chopped (optional)
fresh oregano, finely chopped, to garnish

In a medium bowl, whisk the olive oil with the lemon juice and seasonings. Stir in the beans, onions, and parsley. Toss well.

Garnish the salad with olives and the chopped hard-boiled eggs (omit for vegans), and sprinkle with fresh oregano.

TIP
If you want to reduce the onion flavor in this or any other salad, run the cut onion under cold water, or marinate it in a little vinegar before using it.

Sweet and Sour Cucumber Salad ▼ *Thailand*

One of my daughters introduced me to this lovely Oriental salad in which the light flavor of cucumber is perfectly enhanced by the sweet and sour sauce. Chopped coriander and peanuts add a nice crunch.

Preparation time:
10–15 minutes

SERVES 4

⅔ cup distilled white vinegar
⅔ cup water
½ cup sugar
large pinch of salt
1 large cucumber, peeled
3–4 tablespoons freshly chopped coriander (or flat leaf parsley if preferred)
½ small red onion, chopped
⅓ cup chopped salted peanuts

Mix the vinegar, water, sugar, and salt in a small saucepan and bring it to a boil, stirring to dissolve the sugar. Allow the mixture to reduce and thicken slightly, about 8–10 minutes—it should reduce by about half. Remove the pan from the heat and set the sauce aside to cool. Meanwhile, cut the cucumber into quarters, then slice it thinly across and put the pieces into a bowl.

Once the dressing has cooled, add it to the bowl with half of the chopped coriander or parsley and the onion. Stir the ingredients together well.

Just before serving, stir in the peanuts and garnish with the remaining coriander or parsley.

Cannellini Bean Salad

Seaweed and Cucumber Salad V *Japan*

Preparation time:
15 minutes

Seaweed is a great source of vitamins and minerals, and this salad makes a delicious introduction to it. There are many different types: wakame is dark green, mild flavored, and more akin to a conventional green vegetable. It is sold dried or pickled and can be eaten in salads or soups.

SERVES 4

2 tablespoons dried wakame seaweed, shredded
1 medium cucumber, peeled
3 tablespoons rice or white wine vinegar
2 tablespoons superfine sugar
1–2 tablespoons light soy sauce
2–3 tablespoons sesame seeds, toasted (see tip) to garnish

Soak the wakame in hot water until it is soft and has expanded, about 5 minutes, then drain it thoroughly. If you can't find it already shredded, slice it very finely at this stage.

Halve the cucumber lengthwise, remove the seeds, and slice the lengths thinly to make half-moon shapes.

Mix together the vinegar, sugar, and soy sauce.

Combine the wakame and cucumber in a medium bowl, cover with the dressing, and sprinkle the top with toasted sesame seeds.

TIP
To toast seeds, place them in a small dry frying pan over medium heat. Stir until golden.

Nutty Wild Rice Salad with Citrus Dressing V *USA*

Preparation time:
45–50 minutes

This variation of the classic rice salad is distinguished by the wild rice. If you prefer, you can use a combination of long-grain white and wild rice. Simply cook the two separately and combine them.

SERVES 4

3/4 cup wild rice
3/4 cup hazelnuts, toasted (page 70) and chopped coarsely
6 sun-dried tomatoes, cut into thin strips
juice of 1/2 medium orange
juice of 1/2 lemon
1 small fennel bulb, cubed small
Classic Vinaigrette (page 151), made with garlic
sea salt to taste

In a large saucepan, bring the rice to a boil in 6 cups of water. Simmer uncovered for 45–50 minutes, until the grains are swollen and tender, then drain.

Mix the hazelnuts with the sun-dried tomatoes, orange and lemon juice, and the fennel. Stir the mixture into the cooked rice and toss the salad with sufficient garlic vinaigrette to moisten it. Season to taste with salt.

Seaweed and Cucumber Salad

Creole Spinach and Hot Pepper Salad V *USA*

Preparation time: ***20 minutes***

The deep colors of the spinach, tomatoes, and red pepper mixed with the fiery Creole-style dressing make this salad as vibrant as Southern life itself!

SERVES 4–6

1 pound fresh baby spinach leaves, washed, dried, and the larger leaves torn into small pieces
1 red bell pepper, seeded and cut into thin strips
2 tablespoons scallion, chopped finely
12 cherry tomatoes, halved
Creole Vinaigrette (page 151)
¾ cup Spicy Pecan Mix (page 152)

In a large salad bowl, mix the spinach, red pepper, scallion, and cherry tomatoes. Toss the salad with sufficient vinaigrette to moisten it and sprinkle with the pecans.

Warm Beet Salad with Crème Fraîche V *France*

Preparation time: ***10 minutes***

Cooking time: ***40 minutes***

Freshly cooked beets are a gourmet experience, and serving them warm, as in this salad, brings out the very best of their flavor. (As an alternative, you can make a cold version of this salad—simply peel the raw beets, grate them, and toss them in a bowl with all the other ingredients.)

SERVES 4–6

4 medium beets, unpeeled
1 small red onion, or 3 scallions, chopped finely
4 tablespoons cider vinegar, or white wine vinegar
1 tablespoon superfine sugar (optional)
1 teaspoon Dijon mustard
1 tablespoon olive oil
1 tablespoon freshly chopped parsley
sea salt and black pepper to taste
⅔ cup low-fat crème fraîche, or plain soy yogurt
finely chopped parsley or chives to garnish

Wash the beets and bake them at 350°F until they are tender, about 40 minutes. Allow the beets to cool until they are just warm enough to handle, then peel and grate them coarsely. Place the grated beets in a bowl and mix in the chopped onion.

In a small bowl or jar, combine the vinegar, sugar, mustard, oil, parsley, and salt and pepper to taste, and stir well.

Pour the dressing over the beets and mix well, then fold in the crème fraîche or yogurt. Garnish the salad with chopped parsley or chives.

Creole Spinach and Hot Pepper Salad

Sicilian Bean and Potato Salad V *Italy*

Preparation time: 30 minutes

Simple ingredients are enhanced by the piquant Sicilian flavors of this salad.

SERVES 6

1 pound new potatoes, unpeeled
1 pound green beans, steamed and cut into 1-inch lengths
1 cup cooked or canned haricot (navy) or cannellini (white kidney) beans
1 small red onion, chopped finely
½ cup black olives, pitted and sliced
1–2 tablespoons capers
Classic Vinaigrette (page 151)
2 tablespoons freshly chopped parsley

In a medium saucepan, cook the potatoes in boiling water until they are tender. Allow them to cool slightly and cut them in half.

Mix the potatoes, beans, onion, black olives, and capers in a large bowl.

Pour sufficient vinaigrette over the salad to moisten it and toss well. Sprinkle with parsley and serve.

Warm Puy Lentils on a Bed of Arugula V *France*

Preparation time: 35 minutes

These lentils take their name from Le Puy in central France. They have a delicate flavor and keep their shape and color when cooked. If you can't find Puy lentils, you can use brown or green lentils instead. This salad is equally good warm or cold, and is great for picnics.

SERVES 4–6

⅔ cup Puy lentils, washed and drained
1 large onion, peeled and cut in half
2 cloves garlic, peeled and cut in half
2 bay leaves
5 tablespoons mayonnaise
4 tablespoons crème fraîche, or plain soy yogurt
3 scallions, chopped finely
2 tablespoons finely chopped parsley
sea salt and black pepper to taste
½–¾ cup arugula
½ lemon

In a medium saucepan, cook the lentils with the onion, garlic, and bay leaves in 2½ cups of water. Simmer for 20–25 minutes until the lentils are tender but still slightly nutty. Drain them, and rinse under cold water to cool them a little. Discard the onion, garlic, and bay leaves.

Mix the mayonnaise with the crème fraîche or yogurt, scallions, and parsley. Season to taste with salt and pepper. Fold this sauce into the warm lentils.

Divide the arugula among individual plates, squeeze a little lemon juice over the leaves, and spoon the lentils on top.

Sicilian Bean and Potato Salad

Daikon Salad ~ *Japan*

Crisp daikon (Japanese white radish) makes a wonderful salad mixed with Chinese bok choy and beansprouts. The slight sweetness of some added dates is lovely.

Preparation time:
15 minutes

SERVES 4

1 medium daikon, coarsely grated
1 large carrot, grated
4 large Chinese bok choy, shredded
¾ cup beansprouts
4 dates, stoned and chopped finely
5 tablespoons mayonnaise
½-inch fresh ginger, peeled and grated finely
1 small clove garlic, crushed
soy sauce to taste
freshly chopped coriander (or flat leaf parsley if preferred) to garnish

Combine the prepared salad ingredients in a large bowl.

Mix the mayonnaise with the ginger and garlic, and season to taste with soy sauce.

Fold the dressing into the salad and mix well, before garnishing with chopped coriander or parsley.

TIP
Beansprouts are often soft when you buy them. To make them crisper, soak them in a bowl of ice water for 5 minutes and drain thoroughly before using.

Arugula and Alfalfa Salad V *Italy*

Arugula is a big favorite of mine and this salad is a great way of serving it.

Preparation time:
10 minutes

SERVES 2–4

¼ pound arugula leaves, washed and dried
¼ cup alfalfa sprouts
Classic Vinaigrette (page 151), made with garlic

Mix the arugula and alfalfa sprouts together in a salad bowl. Add sufficient vinaigrette to moisten the salad. Toss and serve at once.

Warm Zucchini Salad V *Greece*

If you love zucchini, you'll enjoy this way of serving it. The salad is particularly delicious with Spanokopitta (page 106).

Preparation time:
15 minutes

SERVES 4

3 young firm zucchini, sliced lengthwise, ⅛ inch thick
2 tablespoons olive oil
1 tablespoon lemon juice
2 tablespoons dill or parsley, chopped
sea salt and black pepper to taste

Steam the sliced zucchini for 3–4 minutes, until tender. Allow it to cool slightly, then place the slices on a serving plate.

Whisk the oil with the lemon juice, dill or parsley, and salt and pepper to taste.

Pour the dressing over the zucchini and serve at once.

Quick and Easy Meals

Pesto Genovese with Green Beans and Potatoes ~ *Italy*

Preparation time:
25 minutes

Fresh pesto has always been one of my favorite pasta sauces because it uses so much delicious basil. In the Italian region of Liguria, pasta is traditionally cooked with potato and green beans, and served with pesto.

SERVES 4–6

6 small waxy new potatoes, unpeeled
3 cups dried penne or fusilli
¾ pound green beans, trimmed and cut into 2-inch lengths
4 tablespoons Pesto Sauce (page 148)
basil leaves to garnish

Boil the potatoes until tender but still firm, for about 15 minutes. When they are cool enough to handle, cut them into small cubes.

Cook the pasta according to the instructions on the package.

Meanwhile, steam the beans until tender but still crisp, for about 5–6 minutes.

Mix the vegetables with the pasta and toss in the pesto. Garnish with basil, and serve immediately with warm ciabatta bread.

Spaghetti alla Putanesca V *Italy*

Preparation time:
15 minutes

Approaching the port of Genoa, sailors claimed they were met by the pungent smell of garlic even before they could see land on the horizon! According to local folklore, the pasta took its name from the prostitutes of the city, who cooked this hearty combination of garlic, capers, and olives.

SERVES 4

¾ pound dried spaghetti
3 tablespoons olive oil
1 red chili pepper, seeded and chopped, (optional)
2 large cloves garlic, sliced finely
20 black olives, pitted, chopped small
2 tablespoons capers, chopped finely
4 tablespoons freshly chopped parsley
black pepper to taste

Cook the spaghetti according to the instructions on the package.

Heat the olive oil in a large saucepan, add the chili pepper and garlic, and cook over medium heat for 2 minutes to soften the garlic.

Add the olives and capers, and stir for a further 2 minutes.

Add the drained spaghetti to the pan and toss it with the sauce, adding the parsley and pepper before serving.

Pesto Genovese with Green Beans and Potatoes

Peasant Pasta Ⓥ *Italy*

This recipe is from my friend Alistair and has become a firm favorite with everyone who has tried it. It is especially good with crusty warm bread, such as ciabatta, and a green salad.

Preparation time:
15 minutes

SERVES 4

3 cups dried conciglie (large pasta shells)
8 tablespoons olive oil
1¾ cups canned butter (lima) beans, drained
2 cloves garlic, sliced thinly
1 teaspoon freshly chopped rosemary
1¾ cups canned artichoke hearts, drained, rinsed, and cut into quarters
sea salt and black pepper to taste
grated vegetarian Parmesan (optional)

Cook the pasta according to the instructions on the package.

Heat the oil in a large frying pan. Fry the butter beans, garlic, and rosemary for about 5 minutes, stirring occasionally, until the beans are lightly browned.

Add the artichokes and heat through. Season to taste with salt and pepper.

Toss the mixture into the hot, drained pasta and serve with grated Parmesan (omit this for vegans).

One Pot Mushroom Risotto Ⓥ *Italy*

This tasty, easy dish has the added bonus of keeping the washing to a minimum!

Preparation time:
25–30 minutes

SERVES 4

4 tablespoons (½ stick) butter or margarine
2 medium onions, chopped
½ pound mushrooms, chopped
1 cup long-grain rice
2½ cups vegetable stock (page 32)
sea salt and black pepper to taste
½ cup frozen peas
1 medium zucchini, sliced thinly
½ cup pine nuts or cashew nuts, toasted (see tip)
4 tablespoons freshly chopped parsley

In a large saucepan, melt the butter or margarine and sauté the onions and mushrooms for 5 minutes.

Add the rice and stir well. Add the stock and seasonings, and bring the mixture to a simmer. Reduce the heat, cover, and cook gently for 10 minutes.

Lay the vegetables on top of the rice and cover again. Let the vegetables steam for 10 minutes. Add more water if the rice begins to dry out.

Stir well and sprinkle with the pine nuts or cashews and the parsley before serving.

TOASTING NUTS

To toast nuts, preheat the oven to 350°F. Lay the nuts on a baking sheet and bake them in the middle of the oven for 15–20 minutes until lightly and evenly golden—timings will depend on the type and size of the nuts. Alternatively, place the nuts on a baking sheet under a preheated broiler or in a dry frying pan over medium heat and brown the nuts, turning them frequently.

Aromatic Vegetable Stir-fry V *China*

Preparation time:
10 minutes

Cooking time:
7 minutes

Fast food can still be healthy food and this stir-fry is lovely served with Special Fried Rice (page 142).

SERVES 4

2 tablespoons peanut oil
½-inch fresh ginger, finely chopped
1 each red, yellow, and green bell pepper, diced
½ cup canned water chestnuts, sliced thinly
¼ cup canned bamboo shoots, sliced
¼ cup snow peas, trimmed
soy sauce to taste

Heat the oil in a wok or frying pan and add the ginger. Stir-fry for about 30 seconds so that it flavors the oil. Add the peppers, stir-fry for a further minute, then add the water chestnuts and bamboo shoots. Stir-fry for a further minute, then add the snow peas and toss for another minute.

Add the soy sauce and remove the wok from the heat. Serve at once.

Spicy Tofu V *Vietnam*

Preparation time:
12 minutes

Tofu (also known as beancurd) is a rich source of protein. Make sure you use the firm not the silken variety for this particular recipe.

SERVES 4

1 tablespoon peanut oil
1 tablespoon finely grated fresh ginger
1 tablespoon finely chopped garlic
1 tablespoon chili bean sauce
2 teaspoons yellow bean sauce
¼ cup vegetable stock (page 32)
2 tablespoons rice wine, or dry sherry
1 teaspoon cornstarch mixed with 2 teaspoons water
1½ pounds firm tofu, drained, patted dry, and cut into ½-inch cubes
sesame oil and finely chopped scallions

Heat a wok over high heat and add the oil. Stir-fry the ginger, garlic, and sauces for 1 minute.

Add the stock and the rice wine or sherry, and simmer gently for 2 minutes.

Stir the blended cornstarch into the mixture. When it has thickened slightly, add the tofu and stir gently. Cook very gently for 2–3 minutes and serve drizzled with a little sesame oil and sprinkled with chopped scallions. Serve with rice, noodles, or in a sandwich.

Overleaf: Oriental Feast (see Menu Planner on page 187)

Sweet and Sour Tofu (V) *Thailand*

Tofu is soybean paste which has been pressed into block form. I love it and enjoy cooking with it. It is versatile, absorbs flavors well, and adds substance to any vegetarian dish.

Preparation time:
30 minutes

SERVES 4–6

SAUCE

1 tablespoon cornstarch
3 tablespoons plus 3/4 cup vegetable stock (page 32)
2 tablespoons white wine vinegar
3 tablespoons sugar
1 tablespoon tomato ketchup
2 tablespoons light soy sauce
1/4 teaspoon cayenne pepper
black pepper to taste
1 tablespoon vegetable oil
1 large clove garlic, chopped finely
1/2-inch fresh ginger, grated

vegetable oil for deep frying
3/4 pound firm tofu, cut into 2-inch rods
soy sauce
2 tablespoons vegetable oil
4 carrots, shredded or cut into ribbons with a potato peeler
8 scallions, shredded

Mix the cornstarch with 3 tablespoons of the stock until smooth.

In a medium bowl, mix together the vinegar, remaining stock, sugar, ketchup, soy sauce, cayenne, and black pepper.

Heat 1 tablespoon of oil gently in a small saucepan, and soften the garlic and ginger. Add the vinegar mixture to the pan and simmer for about 4 minutes. Stir in the cornstarch mixture until the sauce thickens. Check the seasoning.

Pour 2–3 inches of oil into a medium saucepan, and place over medium to high heat. The oil is ready when a cube of bread browns immediately. Deep-fry the tofu for about 5 minutes, until it is golden all over, drain it on paper towels, transfer it to a serving dish, and sprinkle it with soy sauce.

Heat the remaining oil in a wok and stir-fry the carrots and scallions for about 1 minute until they are cooked but still crisp.

Mix the vegetables with the tofu, and pour the sauce over the top.

TIP
Tofu is now readily available in most supermarkets. Look for the marinated and smoked varieties, both of which would work very well in this recipe.

Baked Portobello Mushrooms ~ *USA*

Preparation time:
20 minutes

Cooking time:
20 minutes

Portobello mushrooms have a great depth of flavor, a firm texture and their size makes them ideal for filling.

SERVES 4

4 Portobello or large flat mushrooms, stems removed
4 tablespoons olive oil
juice of 1 lemon
1 clove garlic, chopped
2 teaspoons dried thyme
1 pound spinach leaves, blanched, chopped, and excess moisture squeezed out
½ pound vegetarian Camembert, Brie, or ¼ pound goat's cheese
sea salt and black pepper to taste

Place the mushrooms in a baking dish. Mix the olive oil, lemon juice, garlic, and thyme together, and spoon the mixture over the mushrooms. Bake them in the oven for 10 minutes at 350°F.

Top with the spinach and cheese, and season to taste with salt and pepper. Place under a preheated grill until the cheese has melted, for about 2–3 minutes.

Mozzarella in Carrozza ~ *Italy*

Preparation time:
30 minutes

An Italian obsession, these mozzarella "sandwiches" are dipped in egg and fried until the outside is golden and the inside melts. Serve with a green salad.

SERVES 4

1 loaf of ciabatta, cut into 24 slices
¾ pound mozzarella, sliced thinly
12 slices ripe plum tomatoes, or 12 sun-dried tomatoes
sea salt and black pepper to taste
12 fresh basil leaves
4 large organic eggs
1 teaspoon dried oregano or mixed herbs
⅔ cup milk
olive oil for shallow frying

Cover 12 slices of bread with half of the mozzarella. Place a thin tomato slice, or a sun-dried tomato, on top and season to taste with salt and pepper. Top with a basil leaf. Cover with the remaining mozzarella, and put another slice of bread on top to make a sandwich.

Beat the eggs with the dried herbs and the milk in a large shallow dish. Dip the sandwiches in the egg mixture, turning them once or twice.

Heat ¼ inch of oil in a large frying pan until it is hot. Fry the sandwiches in batches for 2–3 minutes until they are golden on both sides. Drain the sandwiches on paper towels and serve immediately.

Baked Portobello Mushrooms

Rice 'n' Beans ∨ *Caribbean*

Chili heat tempered with coconut milk is the essence of Caribbean cooking. This dish is lovely with a simple avocado and tomato salad, tossed in Classic Vinaigrette made with lime juice (page 151).

Preparation time:
40 minutes

SERVES 4

1 medium onion, chopped finely
2 tablespoons olive oil
½ pound vegetarian burgers, cubed
1 small chili pepper, trimmed and seeded
3 tomatoes, chopped small
2½ cups coconut milk
1½ cups long-grain rice
1 cup canned black-eyed peas or kidney beans, drained
sea salt and black pepper to taste

In a large saucepan, sauté the onion in the olive oil, then add the burger cubes and toss until they are lightly browned.

Add the remaining ingredients, except the beans, and stir well. Bring to a boil. Cover and simmer for 10 minutes. Stir in the beans and cook for a further 10 minutes until the rice is tender, adding water if necessary. Season to taste.

Oriental Fritter ~ *China*

Although this dish is called a fritter, it is really more like a pancake in texture. Once you have got the hang of making these, try them with any combination of your favorite vegetables.

Preparation time:
25–30 minutes

SERVES 2

4 tablespoons all-purpose flour
½ teaspoon sea salt
8 tablespoons water
½ cup tinned straw mushrooms, or tiny button mushrooms, sliced
1 large organic egg, beaten lightly
⅓ cup beansprouts
2 scallions, sliced crosswise
2 tablespoons soy sauce
1 teaspoon sugar
2 tablespoons vegetable oil
1 clove garlic, chopped finely
freshly chopped coriander (or flat leaf parsley if preferred) to garnish

In a large bowl, sift the flour with the salt and stir in the water gradually to make a smooth batter. Add the mushrooms, egg, beansprouts, scallions, soy sauce, and sugar, and stir thoroughly into the batter.

Heat the oil in a medium frying pan and cook the garlic until golden over medium heat. Pour the batter into the pan and allow it to spread. Fry until the underside is crisp and golden. Cut the fritter into four pieces, then turn them over and cook the other side until it is golden and crisp. Serve garnished with a few leaves of coriander or parsley.

Layered Pasta Bake ~ *Greece*

Preparation time: ***20 minutes***

Cooking time: ***20–25 minutes***

This is a lovely dish that my daughter Mary made for me one evening. It goes well with Surfers' Salad (page 57).

SERVES 6

14-ounce can chopped tomatoes
½ cup tomato purée
1 cup water
2 teaspoons dried thyme, or 1 teaspoon fresh, chopped
2 cloves garlic, crushed
10 sun-dried tomatoes, chopped
½ pound vegetarian feta, diced
sea salt and black pepper to taste
3 cups dried pasta (fusilli or penne)
1 medium onion, chopped
3 medium zucchini, sliced
3 tablespoons olive oil
½ cup vegetarian Cheddar, grated
freshly chopped basil to garnish

In a medium saucepan, simmer the tomatoes, tomato purée, and water with the thyme, garlic, and sun-dried tomatoes. When the sauce has reduced and thickened a little, after 8–10 minutes, add the feta. Season to taste with salt and pepper.

Meanwhile, cook the pasta according to the instructions on the package. Drain, and mix it thoroughly with the tomato sauce.

In a medium saucepan, sauté the onion and zucchini in the olive oil for 2–3 minutes.

Spread half of the pasta mixture in a large baking dish and layer the zucchini mixture on top. Cover with the rest of the pasta mixture.

Sprinkle with the Cheddar and bake at 350°F for 20–25 minutes. Serve hot, sprinkled with fresh basil.

Gnocchi with Pumpkin Sauce V *Italy*

Preparation time: ***20 minutes***

Gnocchi are tasty little dumplings made from mashed potato or semolina flour. Most regions of Italy have their own variations.

SERVES 4

1½ pounds pumpkin, diced
1¼ cups dairy or soy milk
1 tablespoon freshly chopped sage or oregano
½ cup dairy or soy cream
sea salt and black pepper to taste
2 x 14-ounce packages fresh gnocchi
¼ cup vegetarian Parmesan, finely grated (optional)
¼ cup hazelnuts, toasted (page 70) and chopped
fresh sage leaves to garnish

In a large saucepan, simmer the pumpkin in the milk with the herbs until tender, about 10 minutes. Add the cream and cook for 1 minute. Season to taste with salt and pepper.

Meanwhile, cook the gnocchi according to the instructions on the package. Toss with the sauce, sprinkle with the Parmesan and hazelnuts, and garnish with sage leaves before serving. Omit the Parmesan for vegans.

Chickpea and Okra Stir-fry **V** *Africa*

This is a truly delicious dish that uses okra, a green vegetable, which is also known as ladies' fingers. If you can't buy okra, zucchini will work just as well.

Preparation time:
25–40 minutes

SERVES 4

2 tablespoons vegetable oil
1 tablespoon butter or margarine
1 large onion, chopped finely
1 clove garlic, crushed
3 tomatoes, chopped
1 green chili pepper, seeded and chopped finely
½-inch fresh ginger, grated
1 pound okra, trimmed
1 teaspoon ground cumin
1 tablespoon freshly chopped coriander (or flat leaf parsley if preferred)
1¾ cups canned chickpeas (garbanzo beans), drained
sea salt and black pepper to taste

In a large frying pan or wok, heat the oil with the butter or margarine. Sauté the onion and garlic for 4–5 minutes until the onion has softened.

Add the tomatoes, chili pepper, and ginger, and stir well, then add the okra, cumin, and coriander or parsley. Cook over medium heat, stirring frequently, then stir in the chickpeas and a little seasoning.

Cook gently for a few minutes longer for the chickpeas to heat through, then spoon into a bowl and serve immediately.

FLAVORED OILS

It is very easy to make your own flavored oils, which you can use for stir-frying, for marinating tofu or vegetables, for salad dressings, or for moistening bread when making sandwiches. Here are a few suggestions, but try experimenting with your own combinations.

Thai—take 3 sprigs of fresh coriander and three 2-inch stems of lemon grass, plus 2 dried red chili peppers. Put them in a clean glass jar or bottle and pour in 2 cups of rapeseed oil or corn oil. Seal the bottle and leave it in a cool, dark place for 2 weeks.

Mexican—place 3 small red chili peppers (with seeds) into a clean glass jar or bottle and pour in 2 cups of sunflower oil. Seal and leave in a cool, dark place for 1 week.

Italian—add 3 sprigs of small fresh basil leaves and 2 cloves of peeled garlic in a clean glass jar or bottle. Pour in 2 cups of extra virgin olive oil. Seal and leave in a cool, dark place for 2 weeks.

French—take 1 sprig of rosemary, 1 sprig of thyme, 1 bay leaf, and 6 black peppercorns. Put them in a clean glass jar or bottle. Pour in 2 cups of extra virgin olive oil and leave in a cool, dark place for about 2 weeks.

Indian—heat 2 tablespoons of olive oil in a pan and add 1 clove of garlic, 1 teaspoon of coriander seeds, 1 teaspoon of cumin seeds, a ½-inch piece of fresh ginger root, finely chopped, and 1 tablespoon of curry paste. Cook over medium heat for about 1 minute. Add 1 cup of olive oil and cook for another 30 seconds. Leave to cool, then transfer to a clean glass jar or bottle.

Chickpea and Okra Stir-fry

Sandwiches

With the stunning selection of breads from around the world that are now available, the humble sandwich has been transformed from an everyday food into something of a gourmet treat! The key to creating a successful sandwich is to experiment and not be afraid to try out new flavors and combinations. Always use the freshest bread available—it is a good idea to slice loaves and rolls on the day you buy them, bag them up, and put them in the freezer until you need them. You don't have to use butter or margarine—try flavored oils (page 80), Pesto (page 148), sun-dried tomato paste, mayonnaise, or a squeeze of lemon juice instead. Here are a few of my favorite combinations to get you started!

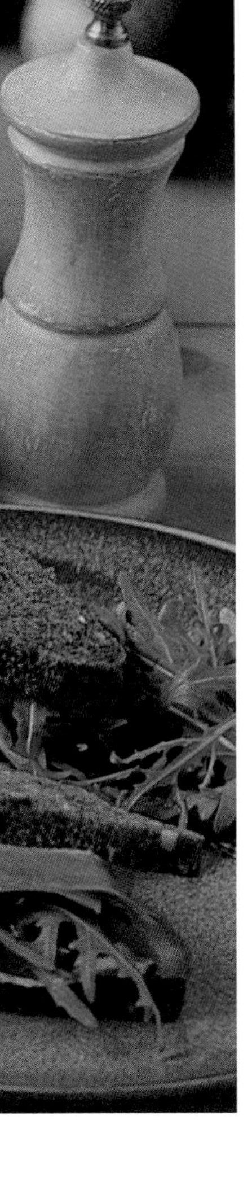

Cold Sandwiches

* Mature vegetarian Cheddar and homemade coleslaw on pumpkin seed bread
* Grated carrot, mayonnaise, Dijon mustard, and arugula on a crusty white roll
* Vegetarian blue cheese with thinly sliced apples and apricot chutney on a poppy seed bagel
* Cottage cheese, thinly sliced red onion, and cucumber with wholegrain mustard in a brown pita bread
* Baby spinach leaves, sliced marinated artichokes, black olives, and feta cheese on light pumpernickel bread
* Cream cheese or mashed tofu with garlic powder and finely chopped tomatoes, parsley, and capers on toasted wholegrain bread
* Thinly sliced tomatoes, avocado, vegetarian mozzarella, and pesto on ciabatta
* Feta, tomato, cucumber, black olives, chopped oregano, and lemon juice on sun-dried tomato bread
* Cooked asparagus mixed with vegetarian blue cheese on walnut bread
* Hummus with sliced pickled beets on pumpernickel
* Vegetarian ham slices with apple chutney, alfalfa sprouts, and shredded lettuce rolled up in an Indian flatbread
* Goat's cheese with spiced fruit chutney on sunflower seed bread
* Vegetarian chicken slices with sliced pickle and lettuce on white bread
* BLT—vegetarian bacon, lettuce, and sliced tomato with mayonnaise on toasted wholegrain bread
* Traditional club sandwich—vegetarian ham and chicken slices, mayonnaise, and lettuce layered between three slices of lightly toasted white bread and served with vegetable chips

Hot Sandwiches

* Croque monsieur—vegetarian ham slices and cheese on white bread, fried in a little hot olive oil and butter until golden brown on both sides
* Sautéed eggplant and onion flavored with mixed herbs, spooned into a baguette, topped with grated cheese, and grilled until bubbling
* Warm oven-roasted vegetables (page 105) with soft goat's cheese on focaccia
* Toasted bagel spread with hummus and topped with capers
* Traditional hot dog with a vegetarian frankfurter served in a split white hot dog roll and topped with fried onions, ketchup, and yellow mustard
* Warmed vegetarian turkey slices with Cranberry Sauce (page 148)

Stir-fried Vegetables with Tofu and Quinoa (V) *China*

Preparation time: 40 minutes

Stir-fries are a brilliant way of cooking a quick and healthy meal. My daughter Heather came up with this inventive combination, but you can vary the vegetables and use whatever is available or in season.

SERVES 4–6

1/3 pound quinoa (see below)
6 tablespoons peanut oil
1/2 pound firm tofu, cubed
1 medium onion, finely chopped
2 large garlic cloves, chopped
2 medium carrots, peeled and grated
1/2 small cauliflower, cut into small florets, blanched
1 medium red bell pepper, seeded and sliced
1 large or 2 small leeks, sliced
2 stalks celery, chopped
1/2 small cabbage, shredded
1 1/2 tablespoons tamari
1 teaspoon dark brown sugar
1 tablespoon fresh lemon juice
1/2 teaspoon ground cinnamon
1/2 teaspoon ground nutmeg
1/2 teaspoon ground cloves
1/2 inch fresh ginger, grated
sea salt and black pepper to taste
1/3 cup sunflower seeds, toasted (page 60)

Rinse the quinoa and put it in a large saucepan with double its volume of cold water. Bring to a boil and cook, uncovered, for 10–15 minutes.

In a large frying pan, heat 2 tablespoons of the oil and fry the tofu until it turns golden all over. Drain it on paper towels and put it to one side.

Heat the remaining oil in a wok. Sauté the onion and garlic, then the carrots, cauliflower, and pepper. Stir-fry over medium heat for 3–4 minutes, then add the leeks, celery, and cabbage. Stir in the tamari, sugar, lemon juice, spices, and fresh ginger. Add the quinoa and continue cooking over medium heat for a further 5 minutes, stirring continuously. Season to taste with salt and pepper. Serve topped with the tofu and sunflower seeds. This is delicious with mango chutney.

QUINOA

Quinoa is something of a wonder grain. It is an ancient crop that is now being rediscovered. It is particularly useful for vegetarians, as it provides more protein than any other grain. It is becoming increasingly available in health food stores, and it is well worth trying to find it. If your local store doesn't stock it, ask—they may be able to order it for you.

MAIN COURSES

Sambhar (Lentil Curry with Vegetables) V *India*

Preparation time:
50 minutes

This great Indian dish is delicious and simple to make. The flavors develop well over twenty-four hours, so it is excellent kept and reheated.

SERVES 4–6

1 cup red lentils, washed
1 tablespoon curry powder
1 teaspoon ground turmeric
8–10 okra, trimmed
2 cups cauliflower florets
½ pound daikon (white radish), peeled and sliced thickly
1 medium onion, sliced thickly
2 teaspoons soft brown sugar
sea salt to taste
4 small tomatoes, quartered
1 red bell pepper, seeded and chopped
3 tablespoons vegetable oil
½ teaspoon mustard seeds
2 whole dried chili peppers
½ teaspoon cumin seeds
2 whole green cardamoms
2 cloves garlic, crushed
fresh coriander (or flat leaf parsley if preferred) to garnish

Place the lentils, curry powder, and turmeric in a large saucepan with enough water to cover them, and bring to a boil. Simmer, covered, until the lentils are mushy, for about 20 minutes. Be careful that they don't dry out: add more water if necessary.

Mash the lentils with a potato masher or wooden spoon and add the okra, cauliflower, daikon, onion, and brown sugar. Add enough water to give the curry the consistency of a thick soup, and simmer it again until the vegetables are tender, about 15–20 minutes. Season to taste with salt. Add the tomatoes and red pepper, cover, and keep the curry warm.

In a small frying pan, heat the oil and fry all the remaining spices and a little salt with the garlic until the mixture crackles. Pour this over the sambhar, and serve garnished with fresh coriander or parsley.

COOKING WITH SPICES

Spices do not deteriorate as quickly as herbs do, but it is still a good idea to buy them whole if possible (i.e. nutmeg, black pepper) and grind them yourself as required, as this will make them last even longer. Whole spices can usually be kept for at least a year, and ground ones will keep for about six months. Always store your spices in airtight jars in a cool, dark, dry place—a spice rack on display in your kitchen may look attractive, but will shorten the life of the spices considerably.

Spicy Peanut Noodles with Satay Cauliflower and Broccoli (V) *Indonesia*

Preparation time:
20–25 minutes

Satay is one of the great classic sauces of the Orient. These spicy noodles are served with steamed broccoli and cauliflower, but they are also excellent with zucchini.

SERVES 6

1½ cups rice noodles
1½ pounds mixed cauliflower and broccoli florets
5 tablespoons sesame oil
2 cups Oriental mushrooms, such as shiitake or oyster
1 tablespoon chunky peanut butter
juice of ½ lime
1 tablespoon yellow bean sauce
1–2 tablespoons soy sauce to taste
1 large clove garlic, chopped finely
½ teaspoon chili powder
6 scallions, cut diagonally into ½-inch pieces
2 tablespoons finely chopped peanuts
1–2 x Satay Sauce (page 148)
fresh coriander (or flat leaf parsley if preferred) to garnish

In a large bowl, soak the rice noodles in warm water according to the instructions on the package. Drain.

Meanwhile, steam the cauliflower and broccoli florets until they are *al dente*, about 5 minutes. In a large frying pan, heat 2 tablespoons of sesame oil over high heat and sauté the mushrooms for 1–2 minutes.

Mix the peanut butter with the lime juice, the remaining sesame oil, yellow bean sauce, soy sauce, garlic, and chili powder. Toss the sauce into the drained noodles, then add the scallions, mushrooms, and peanuts, and toss again.

Pile the noodles onto a large serving plate. Top with the steamed vegetables and satay sauce and garnish with the fresh coriander or parsley.

Chickpea Roast ~ *India*

Preparation time:
25 minutes

Cooking time:
45–50 minutes

This was inspired by my love of Indian food. It goes really well with the Sambhar opposite and Curry Sauce (page 146).

SERVES 4–6

4 large stalks celery, chopped small
½ pound cauliflower, diced small
1¾ cups canned chickpeas (garbanzo beans), drained
1 green pepper, seeded and diced small
¼ cup brown breadcrumbs
1 tablespoon soy sauce
1 tablespoon curry powder, or 1–2 tablespoons Indian curry paste to taste
1 large organic egg, beaten

Steam the celery and cauliflower until tender, for about 6–7 minutes. In a large bowl, mash the chickpeas roughly. Add all of the vegetables.

Stir in the breadcrumbs, add the soy sauce and curry powder to taste, and bind with the egg. Place in a greased 9 x 5 x 3-inch loaf pan.

Bake at 350°F for 45–50 minutes until set. Cool the roast on a rack for at least 20 minutes before turning it out. Cut it into slices using a very sharp knife.

Red Enchiladas ~ *Mexico*

These appetizing tortillas are rolled up around a filling of burger, cheese, and chopped onion, and topped with tomato salsa.

Preparation time: ***25 minutes***

Cooking time: ***10–15minutes***

MAKES 12 (6 SERVINGS)

1¼ cups Salsa (page 151)
⅔ cup tomato purée
⅔ cup water
½ teaspoon each ground cumin and dried oregano
½ pound vegetarian burger, crumbled
vegetable oil for frying
12 large tortillas
2 cups vegetarian Cheddar, grated
1 large red onion, chopped finely
12 black olives, pitted and chopped
1 small iceberg lettuce, shredded
Salsa Verde (page 150), (optional)

In a medium saucepan, mix the salsa with the tomato purée, water, cumin, and oregano, and bring to a boil. Reduce the heat and simmer for 15 minutes, stirring occasionally.

Sauté the burger in 1 tablespoon of oil until lightly browned, and put it to one side. Then, in a large frying pan, lightly fry the tortillas in oil on one side for a few seconds only. Spread 4–6 tablespoons of the sauce over the bottom of a large ovenproof dish. Brush each tortilla with more of the sauce, then fill it with some of the cheese and burger, and ½ tablespoon of the chopped onions, and roll it into a tube. Place the tortilla seamside down in the dish. Repeat with the other tortillas, reserving a little cheese and onion to garnish.

Spoon any remaining red sauce over the tortillas, and sprinkle them with the reserved cheese and onions and the olives. Bake at 350°F for 10–15 minutes. Serve at once, with the shredded lettuce and optional salsa verde.

Mung Bean Stew **V** *Kenya*

This is halfway between a soup and a stew, and is great served with plain boiled rice.

Preparation time: ***1 hour (plus soaking time)***

SERVES 4

1 cup mung beans, soaked for a minimum of 8 hours
2 tablespoons butter, margarine, or ghee
2 cloves garlic, crushed
1 medium red onion, chopped
2 tablespoons tomato purée
½ each green and red bell pepper, seeded and cut into small cubes
1 green chili pepper, seeded and chopped finely
1¼ cups water

Drain the mung beans and put them in a large saucepan. Cover the beans with water, and boil for 30–40 minutes until tender. Remove them from the heat. Mash half with a fork or potato masher and leave the other half whole.

In a medium saucepan, heat the butter, margarine, or ghee, add the garlic and onion and fry until golden brown. Add the tomato purée, the mashed beans and the whole beans, then the peppers. Add the water, and mix well. Cover, and simmer for about 20 minutes. Serve hot.

Red Enchiladas

Creole Vegetable Jambalaya (V) *USA*

Preparation time: 1 hour

Creole cooking followed the path of African peoples to America, where it developed its own character of well seasoned ingredients and spicy sauces. Jambalaya is probably the most famous Creole dish, and cooked this way it is a pleasure to the eye as well as the palate.

SERVES 4–6

3 tablespoons vegetable oil
1 small onion, chopped
1–2 cloves garlic, chopped
3/4 pound vegetarian burger, crumbled
2 vegetarian sausages, defrosted and sliced into rounds
1 medium leek, sliced thinly
1/2 red bell pepper, seeded and sliced
1 stalk celery, sliced
1/4 pound okra, trimmed, or zucchini, diced
1 teaspoon dried thyme
1 tablespoon freshly chopped basil
2 teaspoons Cajun Spice Mix (page 152)
3/4 cup long-grain rice
14-ounce can chopped tomatoes
2 1/2 cups vegetable stock (page 32), or water
3 cups small brown mushrooms, halved
sea salt and black pepper to taste
Tabasco to taste
chopped scallions to garnish

In a large saucepan, heat the oil and soften the onion and garlic over medium heat for 5 minutes. Add the burger and sausages, and fry until browned. Then add the leek, red pepper, celery, and okra or zucchini, and stir until the vegetables have softened slightly. Add the herbs and Cajun spice mix, and stir well. Then stir in the rice until it is thoroughly incorporated.

Add the tomatoes and half of the stock or water, and cook over low heat, covered, for 10–15 minutes. Stir in the mushrooms and remaining stock, and cook for a further 5–10 minutes until the rice is tender.

Season to taste with salt, pepper, and Tabasco. Serve sprinkled with chopped scallions.

RICE

Rice is a staple of the vegetarian diet. It comes in many different varieties, each of which has a different quality, flavor, and aroma. Long-grain is the most widely used type of white rice. It is best suited to dishes where the grains need to remain separate, such as salads and pilafs. Risotto rice, such as arborio, is a plump, short grain which, as its name suggests, is excellent for risottos and other Italian rice dishes. It works well, as it is very starchy and remains moist and sticky. Basmati rice is available in both brown and white. Its delicate aroma makes it ideal for Indian or Thai dishes. Brown rice has a nutty flavor and chewy texture. Wild rice is technically not rice at all, but an aquatic grass grown in America. As it is more expensive than the other varieties, it is often combined with long-grain rice to add a little color and contrast in flavor.

Tacos ⓥ *Mexico*

Preparation time:
1 hour 15 minutes
(plus soaking time)

Crisp taco shells, filled and topped with shredded lettuce, cheese (omit for vegans), and salsa, make a nutritious and quick meal. You can experiment endlessly with fillings. Here are two of my favorites.

Refried Bean Filling

I always make my own refried beans, but you could just as easily buy them in cans.

SUFFICIENT FOR 8–12 TACOS

1 cup pinto beans, soaked for a minimum of 8 hours
2 medium onions, 1 quartered and 1 chopped
4 tablespoons olive oil
½–1 teaspoon chili powder (optional)
sea salt to taste

In a large saucepan, cook the pinto beans with the quartered onion, generously covered with water, until tender, for at least 1 hour. Drain, return them to the pan and mash.

In a small frying pan, fry the onion in the oil with the optional chili powder until it has softened, then add it to the beans. Reheat the beans, stirring, and season to taste with salt.

Spicy Taco Filling

Preparation time:
30 minutes

SUFFICIENT FOR 8–12 TACOS

1 medium onion, chopped finely
2 tablespoons olive oil
½ pound vegetarian burger, crumbled
1 small chili pepper, seeded and chopped, to taste
1 teaspoon ground cumin
½ teaspoon dried oregano
7-ounce can chopped tomatoes, drained
1¾ cups canned kidney beans
sea salt and black pepper to taste

In a medium saucepan, soften the onion in the oil over medium heat for 5 minutes. Add the burger, chili pepper, cumin, and oregano, and simmer gently for 5 minutes, then add the tomatoes and beans, and simmer gently for another 5 minutes, stirring occasionally. Season to taste with salt and pepper.

Allow 2–3 taco shells per person. Spoon in a generous dollop of your chosen filling and top with shredded lettuce, grated cheese, and/or sour cream or soy yogurt, and Salsa (page 151).

Deep Dish Pie V *UK*

Preparation time:
45 minutes

Cooking time:
40 minutes

Savory pie served with a mound of fluffy mashed potatoes is a British institution.

SERVES 6

2 medium onions, chopped
1 clove garlic, chopped
2 tablespoons vegetable oil
½ pound mushrooms, chopped
1 pound vegetarian chunks or burgers, cubed
1 teaspoon fresh thyme
4 cups Special Gravy (page 149), or made from vegetarian gravy mix
2 tablespoons soy sauce
1 tablespoon balsamic vinegar
sea salt and black pepper to taste
¾ pound puff pastry
beaten organic egg or soy milk to glaze

In a large saucepan, fry the onions and garlic in the oil over medium heat for about 4 minutes. Add the mushrooms and toss well.

Add the chunks or cubed burgers, and the thyme. Cook for 5 minutes over low heat. Add the gravy and simmer gently for 15–20 minutes until it has thickened. Add the soy sauce and balsamic vinegar, and season to taste with salt and pepper. Set it aside to cool. Place a ceramic pastry support, if you have one, in the center of a large pie dish, then spoon in the filling.

Roll out the pastry ¼ inch thick to the shape of the dish. Cut a strip ¾ inch wide from around the edge of the pastry. Continue rolling the main piece of pastry until it fits the dish once more. Dampen the rim of the dish with water, and place the pastry strip around it. Moisten the attached pastry strip, then cover the pie with the pastry lid. Press the edges together firmly and trim the excess pastry. Use the back of a knife to make a decorative edge. You can also roll out the trimmings to make pastry leaves (see photograph opposite). Brush the pastry lid with beaten egg or milk.

Bake the pie in the oven at 450°F until the pastry has risen and turned lightly golden, for about 10–12 minutes. Reduce the heat to 400°F and cook for a further 20–25 minutes until crisp and golden brown. Serve at once with Special Gravy and Special Mashed Potatoes (page 129).

eep Dish Pie with
pecial Mashed Potatoes
nd Special Gravy

Pad Thai Noodles ⓥ *Thailand*

Preparation time:
30 minutes

This dish combines all the tastes that the Thais cherish in their cuisine—sweet, sour, and hot.

SERVES 4

⅔ cup rice ribbon noodles
peanut oil for frying
⅔ cup firm tofu, cut into slim rods
4 cloves garlic, chopped finely
1 large organic egg, beaten (optional)
4 tablespoons vegetable stock (page 32)
2 tablespoons fresh lime juice
1 tablespoon sugar
2 tablespoons soy sauce
1 teaspoon sea salt
½ teaspoon dried chili flakes
¾ cup peanuts, chopped
1 pound beansprouts
3 scallions, the whites cut thinly across, the greens sliced into thin lengths
2 limes or 1 lemon, quartered lengthwise, to garnish

In a medium bowl, soak the rice noodles in warm water according to the instructions on the package. Meanwhile, prepare all the other ingredients so that they are ready when you start stir-frying. Heat about 1 inch of the oil in a large wok and fry the tofu over medium heat, turning the pieces until they are golden all over. Remove them with a slotted spoon and drain on paper towels.

Omit the following stage if you are not using the egg and go straight to *. Pour all but approximately 1 tablespoon of oil from the wok and heat until sizzling. Add the beaten egg, and scramble it lightly. Remove it from the wok and put to one side. *Heat a further 2 tablespoons of oil, add the garlic and drained noodles, and toss until they are coated with oil. Add the stock, lime juice, sugar, and soy sauce, and toss well, gently pushing the noodles around the pan. Then add the tofu, egg, salt, chili flakes, and half of the peanuts, and turn the noodles again. Finally, add all but a handful of the beansprouts and the scallions. Turn for a further minute or two, until the beansprouts have softened slightly.

Arrange the noodles on a warm serving plate and garnish with the remaining peanuts and beansprouts. Place the lime and/or lemon wedges around the edge.

NOODLES

Noodles are becoming increasingly popular and offer an interesting alternative to rice or pasta. There are many different types—wheat, potato, or rice flour, and those made from soy or mung bean starch. Dried noodles are now available in most supermarkets and the fresh ones can be found in specialist Chinese or Japanese food shops. Egg noodles are made from wheat flour and egg and sold in flat sheets that separate when cooked. They are, of course, unsuitable for a vegan diet. Cellophane or glass noodles are made from ground mung bean flour and, although beautiful to look at, have a gelatinous texture that takes a little getting used to! Rice noodles—also known as rice vermicelli—are long, thin white strands. Ribbon noodles are made from ground rice and water. These are broad noodles that need to be soaked before cooking. As a general rule you should allow ⅓–½ cup of dried noodles per person.

Golden Pumpkin Curry ♥ *India*

Preparation time:
30–35 minutes

Pumpkin is one of my favorites. This warming, nourishing way of serving it is great with a bowl of basmati rice and warm naan bread.

SERVES 4

2 tablespoons vegetable oil or ghee
½ teaspoon mustard seeds
2 large onions, sliced
4 cloves garlic, crushed
½-inch fresh ginger, peeled and grated
2 green chili peppers, seeded and chopped
1 teaspoon turmeric powder
1 pound pumpkin, peeled, seeded, and cubed
sea salt to taste
1 teaspoon sugar
⅔ cup vegetable stock (page 32), or water
freshly chopped coriander (or flat leaf parsley if preferred) to garnish

In a medium saucepan, heat the oil or ghee and fry the mustard seeds for 1 minute over medium heat. Then add the onions, garlic, ginger, and chili peppers. Stir-fry for 5 minutes.

Add the turmeric and mix well, then add the pumpkin, a little salt, and the sugar, and mix thoroughly. Cook gently, covered, for 10 minutes, stirring occasionally.

Then add the stock or water and continue to cook until the pumpkin is tender, for about another 5–10 minutes. Serve sprinkled with coriander or parsley.

Risotto Milanese ~ *Italy*

Preparation time:
35 minutes

Risotto Milanese is a classic dish—its simplicity is its charm. Serve it with the best Italian bread you can find and a simple tomato and red onion salad.

SERVES 4

1 medium red onion, chopped
6 tablespoons (¾ stick) butter or margarine
1 tablespoon olive oil
1¼ cups risotto or arborio rice
pinch of saffron strands
½ cup dry white wine
5 cups vegetable stock (page 32), warmed
½ cup vegetarian Parmesan, grated
sea salt and black pepper to taste

In a large saucepan, soften the onion in half of the butter or margarine and all of the oil over medium heat for about 5 minutes. Add the rice, and stir until it is thoroughly incorporated with the onion. Add the saffron and the wine. Add the warmed vegetable stock a ladle at a time, stirring constantly, adding more stock as the rice cooks and absorbs most of the liquid.

After 20 minutes, taste the rice. It should be tender in the center of the grain. Cook for a further 5 minutes if necessary. Stir in the Parmesan and the remaining butter or margarine. Season to taste with salt and pepper.

Fontina and Tomato Pie ~ *Italy*

This beautiful looking dish from Piedmont in northern Italy is perfect for special occasions. If you can't find Fontina, use vegetarian Cheddar or a similar waxy cheese.

Preparation time: ***30 minutes***

Cooking time: ***20–30 minutes***

SERVES 6

15–20 slices focaccia or crusty white bread, cut about 1/2 inch thick
2/3 cup dairy or soy milk
2 tablespoons olive oil
1 medium red onion, sliced thinly
1 small yellow bell pepper, seeded and chopped
sea salt and black pepper to taste
2 cups Fontina cheese, grated
1/2 pound tomatoes, sliced thinly
4 large organic eggs
1/2 cup grated vegetarian Parmesan
1 tablespoon freshly chopped oregano

Dip the bread slices into the milk to soften, then line a buttered 9-inch ovenproof dish with them, making a scalloped edge with the crusts. Bake for 15–20 minutes at 400°F until lightly golden.

In a medium frying pan, sauté the onion and yellow pepper in the oil until soft. Season to taste with salt and pepper, and spoon the filling over the bread. Sprinkle with grated cheese, and cover with the tomatoes.

Beat the eggs with the Parmesan and oregano, and pour them over the pie filling. Return it to the oven and bake for a further 20–30 minutes until the eggs have set.

Boston Slow-Baked Beans Ⓥ *USA*

Preparation time: ***1 hour (plus soaking time)***

Cooking time: ***4 hours***

SERVES 4–6

1 pound dried haricot (navy) beans, soaked for a minimum of 8 hours
2 tablespoons soft brown sugar
4–6 tablespoons dark molasses
1 tablespoon dry mustard
1 medium onion, chopped
1 clove garlic
4 tablespoons vegetarian Worcestershire sauce
4 tablespoons tomato purée
1 3/4 cups vegetable stock (page 32)
2 cups tomato juice
sea salt and black pepper to taste

Drain the beans and place them in a large flameproof casserole with enough water to cover them. Bring to a boil and boil rapidly for 10 minutes, then simmer, covered, for 45 minutes.

Drain the beans and return them to the casserole with the remaining ingredients. Mix thoroughly, season with salt and pepper to taste, cover, and bake in the oven at 300°F for 4 hours until the beans are tender.

Check and stir the beans occasionally during cooking and add a little water, if necessary, to prevent them from drying out. Taste and adjust the seasoning if necessary before serving.

Fontina and Tomato Pie

Goulash V *Hungary*

Hungary's most famous dish is comfort food at its best. There is nothing fashionable about it—it has stood the test of time because it is simply great food. I usually serve it with rice or Dumplings (page 152).

Preparation time: ***1 hour***

SERVES 6

2 tablespoons olive oil
1 large onion, chopped
2 medium carrots, peeled and sliced
1 medium parsnip, peeled and cubed
¾ pound vegetarian chunks or burgers, cubed
1–2 tablespoons paprika to taste
14-ounce can tomatoes
3 tablespoons tomato purée
1 teaspoon caraway seeds
2½ cups vegetable stock (page 32)
2 medium potatoes, diced
sea salt and black pepper to taste
1 cup crème fraîche, or warmed soy cream
paprika and finely chopped parsley to garnish

In a large saucepan, heat the olive oil and fry the onion, carrots, and parsnip over medium heat until they begin to brown, about 8 minutes.

Add the vegetarian chunks or burgers, paprika, tomatoes, tomato purée, and caraway seeds. Heat gently and stir for 3–5 minutes.

Add the stock or water and the potatoes, and mix well. Bring to a simmer, cover, and cook for a further 25–30 minutes until the potatoes are tender, adding more stock or water if necessary.

Season to taste with salt and pepper. Stir in the crème fraîche or soy cream, heat it through gently, and garnish with a dusting of paprika and a sprinkling of parsley.

TIP

Use Hungarian paprika if you can find it. Some types of commercial paprika are only coloring agents and won't give you the desired authentic flavors.

Quesadillas ~ *Mexico*

Preparation time:
20 minutes

Cooking time:
5 minutes

Folded tortillas that contain various fillings are classic Mexican food. You can experiment using any kind of filling you choose.

MAKES 6

1 tablespoon vegetable oil
1 small onion, chopped
½ pound vegetarian burger, crumbled
4 tablespoons freshly chopped coriander (or flat leaf parsley if preferred)
1–2 tablespoons vegetable stock (page 32)
6 large tortillas
⅔ pound vegetarian Cheddar, grated
12 thin slices of tomato
12 thin slices of red onion
6 tablespoons Salsa (page 151)
½ iceberg lettuce, shredded
1 large ripe avocado, diced
1 tablespoon lemon juice
6 tablespoons sour cream or plain soy yogurt
4 scallions, chopped finely

In a medium frying pan, heat the oil and sauté the onion and burger until lightly browned. Add half the coriander or parsley and the stock, and cook for 2–3 minutes.

Cover half of each tortilla with grated cheese, two slices of tomato and onion, and some burger. Fold the tortillas over, transfer them to a baking sheet, top with a little salsa, and bake at 400°F for about 5 minutes, until the cheese melts.

Meanwhile, mix the shredded lettuce with the avocado and lemon juice.

Spoon some sour cream or yogurt on top of each tortilla, sprinkle with chopped scallions and the remaining coriander or parsley, and serve at once, with the avocado mixture on the side.

Sauerkraut and Sausages Ⓥ *Germany*

Preparation time:
1 hour 55 minutes

SERVES 6–8

2 large onions, sliced
2 tablespoons vegetable oil
2 pounds canned sauerkraut
4 large carrots, sliced
12 juniper berries, crushed
1¼ cup vegetable stock (page 32)
16 vegetarian sausages, grilled until well browned

In a large flameproof casserole dish, soften the onions in the oil gently over low to medium heat for about 10 minutes. Add the sauerkraut and the carrots, toss together well, then add the juniper berries.

Stir in the stock and simmer, covered, for 1½ hours. Add a little water if necessary to keep the mixture moist during cooking.

Add the sausages just before serving, mix them in well, and serve with a big bowl of Special Mashed Potatoes (page 129).

Vegetable Kichdi V *India*

Preparation time:
40 minutes

This wonderful Indian dish is aromatic and beautifully spiced. Serve it with Yogurt with Fresh Mint (page 147) and warm naan bread.

SERVES 4–6

1 cup basmati rice
⅓ cup red lentils
2 tablespoons butter, margarine, or ghee
2 red chili peppers, seeded and chopped
1 tablespoon cumin seeds
5 peppercorns, crushed
4 whole green cardamoms
4 cloves
1-inch stick cinnamon
1 teaspoon turmeric powder, or a pinch of saffron strands
2 large onions, chopped finely
2 inches fresh ginger, grated
1 large potato, peeled and diced
1 large tomato, skinned and chopped
¼ cup frozen peas
½ cup each cauliflower and broccoli florets
sea salt
2½ cups water
cashew nuts, toasted (page 70), to garnish

Rinse the rice with the lentils in a large sieve.

In a large frying pan, heat the butter, margarine, or ghee, and fry the spices with over medium heat. When they sizzle and crackle, add the chopped onions and ginger, and fry until golden brown.

Next, add the prepared vegetables, rice, lentils, and salt, and stir in the water. Stir and simmer for approximately 15–20 minutes until the rice is cooked, adding more water if necessary. Stir and serve sprinkled with the cashew nuts.

Grilled Spicy Tofu V *Senegal*

Preparation time:
15–20 minutes
(plus marinating time)

A very unusual dish from Senegal with tempting flavors and textures.

SERVES 4–6

½ cup chunky peanut butter
3 tablespoons peanut oil
¼ cup lemon juice
2 large onions, chopped
2 chili peppers, chopped
2 cloves garlic, chopped
2 sprigs of thyme, chopped finely
1 bay leaf, crumbled
2 large canned pimientos, cut into strips
sea salt and black pepper to taste
1 pound firm tofu, cut into ½-inch cubes

In a large flameproof dish, combine the peanut butter, peanut oil, half of the lemon juice, the onions, chili peppers, garlic, thyme, bay leaf, and the pimientos. Season to taste with salt and pepper. Place the tofu in this marinade and leave it for at least 30 minutes.

Preheat the broiler to high for 5 minutes.

Place the dish of marinated tofu under the grill until it has browned on top. Turn and brown again, then twice more until the tofu is golden brown all over. Serve with rice.

Vegetable Kichdi

Banana and Yam Stew ⓥ *Tanzania*

Preparation time: 1 hour 15 minutes

SERVES 6

2/3 cup peanut oil
2 pounds yams, peeled and cubed
1 green chili pepper, seeded and chopped
1 tablespoon freshly chopped coriander
1 medium red onion, chopped
1 large tomato, skinned and quartered
1 large carrot, diced
2 cloves garlic, chopped
1 teaspoon each ground cloves, turmeric, and cumin
sea salt and black pepper to taste
1 1/4 cups coconut milk
5 cups vegetable stock (page 32)
2 bay leaves
1 tablespoon cornstarch, mixed with 2 tablespoons cold water
2 green bananas, peeled and sliced

In a large saucepan, heat the oil and sauté the yam pieces over medium heat until they are golden brown. Remove them from the pan with a slotted spoon.

Reduce the heat and in the same oil sauté the chili pepper, coriander, onion, tomato, carrot, garlic, and cloves with the spices. Season to taste with salt and pepper.

Add the coconut milk and the stock, and bring to a boil. Add the bay leaves, then lower the heat to a simmer. Stir in the cornflour mixture.

Add the yams and bananas, and season to taste with salt and pepper. Cover and simmer gently for 30 minutes. Check the seasoning, then allow the stew to sit for 10 minutes and remove the bay leaves before serving it with rice.

COCONUT MILK

Coconut milk can be bought ready to use or made from creamed, fresh, or dried coconut. The liquid inside a coconut is a thin, sweet, and rather watery fluid, and should not be confused with coconut milk as a cooking ingredient.

Green Curry ⓥ *Thailand*

If you are in a hurry, you can buy Thai green curry paste, but it is worth making your own if you can. Serve with rice.

Preparation time: 35–40 minutes

SERVES 2–3

2 tablespoons vegetable or peanut oil
1–2 tablespoons Green Curry Paste (page 149)
1 1/4 cups coconut milk
1 small eggplant, cubed
8-ounce can bamboo shoots, drained
1 medium onion, diced
1 tablespoon superfine sugar
1 teaspoon soy sauce
1 medium zucchini, cubed
chopped coriander (or flat leaf parsley if preferred) to garnish

In a medium saucepan, heat the oil over medium heat and stir in the curry paste for a few seconds. Gradually add the coconut milk and heat it through, mixing well, for 3 minutes. Add the eggplant, bamboo shoots, and onion, and stir gently for 5 minutes. Stir in the sugar and soy sauce, and mix well.

Bring the mixture to a boil, then simmer gently for 10 minutes, adding a little water to moisten it if necessary. Add the zucchini and cook for a further 5 minutes. Remove the pan from the heat and let it sit for a few minutes.

Transfer the curry to a bowl and sprinkle with chopped coriander or parsley.

Bean and Sweet Potato Nachos ~ *Mexico*

Preparation time:
1 hour 15 minutes

These substantial nachos are not as complicated as they may look at first glance and are well worth a try.

SERVES 4

1½ pounds sweet potato, peeled and diced
3 tablespoons olive oil
2 teaspoons cumin seeds
2 teaspoons coriander seeds
1 medium onion, sliced thinly
2 cloves garlic, crushed
1 small red chili pepper, seeded and chopped finely
1 teaspoon paprika
14-ounce can chopped tomatoes
½ each medium red and green bell pepper, seeded and diced
1¼ cups canned red kidney beans, rinsed and drained
½ pound tortilla (corn) chips
2 cups vegetarian Cheddar, grated
2 tablespoons freshly chopped coriander (or flat leaf parsley if preferred)
1 medium avocado, peeled, stoned and sliced
½ cup sour cream or plain soy yogurt

In a large baking dish, mix the sweet potato, 2 tablespoons of the oil, and the spices. Bake, uncovered, at 350°F for 50–60 minutes, until tender.

Heat the remaining oil gently in a pan and add the onion, garlic, chili pepper, and paprika. Cover, and cook until the onion is soft, about 10 minutes, stirring occasionally. Add the tomatoes with their juices and the peppers, and simmer uncovered for 5 minutes. Stir in the beans.

Divide the corn chips among four individual ovenproof dishes and top with the bean mixture, then with the sweet potato, and finish with the cheese. Bake for 10 minutes until the nachos are well heated and the cheese has melted.

Serve sprinkled with coriander or parsley, with avocado and sour cream or yogurt served separately.

Minted Couscous with Roasted Vegetables

V *Morocco*

Couscous, traditional Berber food, is one of North Africa's great dishes. Here, mixed with lemon juice and mint and served with roasted vegetables, it makes a memorable meal.

Roasted Vegetables

Preparation time: 20 minutes (plus marinating time)

Cooking time: 30–35 minutes

SERVES 4

1 large eggplant, cut into chunky sticks
1 pound zucchini, cut into chunky sticks
1 large red onion, cut into 8 wedges
12 cloves garlic, in their skins
10 basil leaves, torn roughly
1 sprig of rosemary, chopped
4–6 tablespoons olive oil
1 each red and yellow bell pepper, grilled, skinned, quartered, and seeded
4 mushrooms, sliced
15–20 black olives, pitted

Put the prepared eggplant, zucchini, onion, and garlic into a large bowl with the basil and rosemary. Sprinkle with half the olive oil and toss well. Let it sit at room temperature for 3–4 hours.

Preheat the oven to 425°F. Spread the vegetables on a baking sheet or sheets, in a single layer, and drizzle with the remaining olive oil. Roast them for 15 minutes, then add the peppers, mushrooms, and olives, and toss. Return the vegetables to the oven and roast them for a further 10–15 minutes until they are tender, turning once more before the end of the cooking time.

Minted Couscous

Preparation time: 20 minutes

SERVES 4

1 cup couscous
2½ cups water, boiled
⅔ cup olive oil
juice and grated zest of 2 lemons
1 yellow bell pepper, seeded and chopped finely
4 scallions, chopped finely
4–6 tablespoons freshly chopped mint
sea salt and black pepper to taste

Put the couscous into a large bowl and pour the boiling water over it. Stir for a couple of minutes and leave it until the water has absorbed and the couscous is tender, for about 6–7 minutes.

Add the olive oil, lemon juice, and zest, and mix them in thoroughly.

Stir in the chopped pepper, scallions, and mint. Season to taste with salt and pepper, and serve with the roasted vegetables.

Minted Couscous with Roasted Vegetables

Spanokopitta ~ *Greece*

This classic Greek dish combines crisp filo pastry with spinach, leeks, and dill. Serve with Cephalonian Salad (page 55).

Preparation time:
40 minutes

Cooking time:
45–50 minutes

SERVES 6–8

1 pound leeks, washed and sliced thinly
6 tablespoons olive oil
2 pounds fresh spinach, washed and trimmed, or 1 pound frozen spinach
½ pound vegetarian feta cheese
3 large organic eggs, beaten
⅔ cup dairy or soy milk
1 tablespoon freshly chopped dill or fennel
½ teaspoon nutmeg
sea salt and black pepper to taste
8 scallions, sliced
¾ cup pine nuts, toasted (page 70)
½ pound filo pastry

In a large frying pan, sauté the leeks in 2 tablespoons of olive oil until they soften. In a large saucepan, wilt the spinach over high heat, drain it thoroughly in a colander, and squeeze out the excess water.

In a large bowl, mash the feta with a fork and add the beaten eggs, milk, dill or fennel, and nutmeg, and season well with salt and pepper. Add the prepared spinach, leeks, scallions, and pine nuts, and fold these into the mixture.

Grease a 9-inch square baking pan and line it with half of the pastry sheets. To do this, lay them down one at a time, brushing each one with olive oil. Next, spread the filling evenly over the pastry base. To finish, layer the remaining pastry sheets on top, again brushing each one liberally with the olive oil, especially the last sheet.

Bake at 375°F for 40–45 minutes, until the top of the pie is golden and crisp. Allow it to cool a little before cutting it into squares with a sharp knife.

Traditional Artichoke Pie ~ *Italy*

Preparation time: **25 minutes**

Cooking time: **40–45 minutes**

This is a classic Italian party dish *par excellence*—as beautiful to look at as it is to eat. Serve it either hot or warm, with a choice of salads.

SERVES 6–8

2 tablespoons (1/4 stick) butter or margarine
1/2–3/4 cup olive oil
2 x 14-ounce cans artichoke hearts, drained and cut in half
4 1/2 cups mushrooms, sliced
2 tablespoons freshly chopped parsley
1 clove garlic, crushed
1 cup ricotta cheese
3 large organic eggs
4 tablespoons vegetarian Parmesan cheese, grated
1/2 teaspoon ground nutmeg
sea salt and black pepper to taste
1/2 pound filo pastry
1/2 cup hazelnuts, toasted (page 70) and

In a large frying pan, heat the butter or margarine with 2 tablespoons of oil and cook the artichokes, mushrooms, parsley, and garlic gently for 5 minutes over medium heat. Set it aside.

Mix the ricotta with the eggs and Parmesan in a large bowl. Season to taste with nutmeg, salt, and pepper.

Grease a 9-inch square baking pan and line it with half of the pastry sheets. To do this, lay them down one at a time, brushing each one with olive oil.

Spread the artichoke and mushroom mixture over the pastry, followed by the ricotta mixture. Scatter the toasted hazelnuts on top.

To finish, layer the remaining pastry sheets on top, again brushing each one liberally with the olive oil, especially the last sheet. Bake at 350°F for 40–45 minutes until the top has puffed up and turned golden.

Overleaf: Greek Menu (see Menu Planner on page 184)

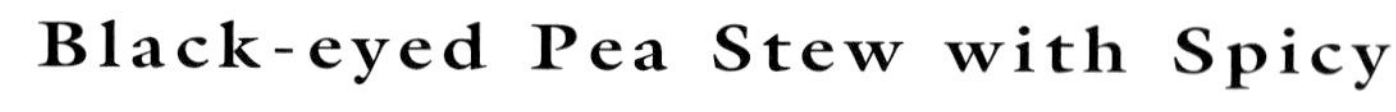

Black-eyed Pea Stew with Spicy Pumpkin V *Africa*

This dish is, in fact, two stews served together. Invest a little time and effort, and your reward will be a hearty, intensely flavored meal.

Preparation time:
30 minutes

SERVES 4

BLACK-EYED PEA STEW

1 large onion, chopped
2 large carrots, sliced
1 green or red bell pepper, seeded and chopped
2 cloves garlic, chopped
1 tablespoon freshly chopped or 1 teaspoon dried thyme
1 teaspoon paprika
½ teaspoon mixed spice
4 tablespoons peanut oil
1¼ cups vegetable stock (page 32)
2 x 14-ounce cans black-eyed peas
sea salt and black pepper to taste
Tabasco to taste

SPICY PUMPKIN

2 tablespoons (¼ stick) butter or margarine
1½ pound pumpkin, cubed
1 medium onion, chopped
2 cloves garlic, crushed
3 tomatoes, skinned and chopped
1 teaspoon ground cinnamon
2 teaspoons curry powder
pinch of grated nutmeg
1¼ cups water
sea salt and black pepper to taste

To make the black-eyed pea stew, sauté the onion, carrots, pepper, garlic, thyme, and spices in the oil in a large saucepan for 5 minutes. Add the stock, bring to a boil, reduce the heat to a simmer, stir in the black-eyed peas, and season to taste with salt, pepper, and Tabasco. Cover and simmer for 15 minutes, adding more stock or water as necessary until the vegetables are tender.

To make the spicy pumpkin, melt the butter or margarine in a large saucepan over medium heat. Add the pumpkin, onion, garlic, tomatoes, spices, and water. Stir well and simmer, covered, until the pumpkin is tender, about 10–15 minutes. Season to taste with salt and pepper. Serve with the black-eyed peas and a dish of rice or couscous.

PUMPKIN

Pumpkins are native to America but have been known in Britain since the sixteenth century. I grow them very successfully in my own garden! They can grow to an enormous size and many pumpkins are larger than the average household might want, so it is well worth having more than one recipe up your sleeve before you buy one. As well as the traditional pumpkin pie, I use my own crop to make delicious soups and risottos, or I oven roast chunks with other winter vegetables. It is useful to remember that pumpkin contains a lot of water and will cook down to approximately half its bulk.

Black-eyed Pea Stew with Spicy Pumpkin

Party Nut Loaf ~ *UK*

This fabulous loaf looks wonderful and slices very well, even when hot. It is a great party dish served with the Roasted Red Pepper Sauce (page 149).

Preparation time: **45 minutes**

Cooking time: **40 minutes**

SERVES 8

8 tablespoons (1 stick) butter or margarine
1 large onion, chopped finely
1½ tablespoons all-purpose flour
4–5 tablespoons dairy or soy milk
3 large organic eggs, separated
1½ cup unsalted cashew nuts, ground finely
1¼ cup brazil nuts, ground finely
1¾ cups dried brown breadcrumbs
½ cup mature vegetarian Cheddar, grated
1 tablespoon freshly chopped parsley

FILLING

4 shallots, chopped
1 cup mushrooms, chopped
1 medium zucchini, grated
1 teaspoon each freshly chopped thyme, rosemary, and sage
2 tablespoons each freshly chopped parsley and chives
¼ teaspoon ground nutmeg
sea salt and black pepper to taste

Butter a 6 x 10-inch loaf pan and line it with well-greased wax paper.

In a medium saucepan, melt 2 tablespoons of the butter or margarine and soften the onion over medium heat for about 5 minutes. Stir in the flour and cook for a further minute. Gradually add the milk, stirring continuously until the mixture thickens. Simmer for 2 minutes, then remove the pan from the heat. Cool, then beat in the egg whites (put the yolks to one side for the filling), nuts, breadcrumbs, cheese, and parsley, and mix well. Put this aside until you have prepared the filling.

To make the filling, cook the shallots in the remaining butter or margarine in a medium pan until soft, then add the mushrooms and cook over high heat until browned. Add the zucchini to the pan and cook over medium heat for 2–3 minutes until the juices run, then add the herbs and nutmeg. Season to taste with salt and pepper and remove the pan from the heat. Allow the pan to cool slightly, then stir in the egg yolks.

Spread half of the nut mixture into the loaf pan, spoon the mushroom and zucchini filling on top, and cover with the remaining nut mixture.

Bake at 350°F for 40 minutes or until firm. Let it stand for 10 minutes before turning the loaf out onto a serving plate and slicing it with a very sharp knife.

Festive Loaf ~ *USA*

Preparation time:
15 minutes

Cooking time:
40–45 minutes

The simplicity of this loaf is as appealing as its delicious flavors and textures. Served with all the trimmings, it is a fitting centerpiece for any festive occasion.

SERVES 8

4 tablespoons olive oil
2 medium onions, chopped
16 vegetarian burgers, defrosted and crumbled
2 tablespoons each freshly chopped sage and rosemary
4 large organic eggs, beaten
6 tablespoons soy cream
4 tablespoons tamari or soy sauce

In a large frying pan, heat the olive oil and sauté the onions until soft. Add the crumbled burgers and brown them with the onions, taking care that they do not stick to the pan. Add the herbs and fry for a further 2 minutes before removing the pan from the heat.

Place the mixture in a bowl and add the beaten eggs, soy cream, and tamari or soy sauce. Mix well, then press it into a well-greased loaf pan and bake at 350°F for 40–45 minutes until it has set in the center.

Leave the loaf in the pan to cool, and turn it out carefully after 15 minutes. Serve warm, with Special Gravy (page 149) or Onion and Juniper Gravy (page 151), Cranberry Sauce (page 148), and Herby Stuffing (page 153).

Quiche Linda ~ *France*

Preparation time:
40 minutes

Cooking time:
30 minutes

My version of a French classic, this quiche rises beautifully and is exquisitely light and fluffy. Serve with Fennel and Arugula Salad (page 50).

SERVES 6

½ pound shortcrust pastry (page 153)
1 large onion, chopped
6 slices vegetarian bacon, chopped
1 tablespoon olive oil
4 large organic eggs, beaten
1½ cups vegetarian Cheddar, grated
sea salt and black pepper to taste
⅔ cup dairy or soy milk, or dairy or soy cream

Roll out the pastry thinly, line a 9-inch quiche dish and bake blind (page 161). Set the pie shell aside to cool.

Meanwhile, in a medium frying pan, sauté the onion and bacon in the oil for 2–3 minutes, stirring until the onion is soft and the bacon is golden.

Whisk the eggs until foamy and fold in the onion, bacon, and grated cheese. Season to taste with salt and pepper. Finally, add the milk or cream. Pour the mixture into the pie shell.

Bake at 400°F for 30 minutes, until it puffs up and rises well. Serve immediately.

Asparagus and Lemon Risotto V *Italy*

To get the best flavors from this dish, use fresh, young asparagus.

Preparation time: 40 minutes

SERVES 4–6

3 tablespoons olive oil
2 shallots, chopped
1 clove garlic, chopped finely
1 stalk celery, chopped small
1¼ cups risotto or arborio rice
3½ cups vegetable stock (page 32), warmed
1 bunch asparagus, trimmed and chopped into 2-inch pieces
6 fresh sage leaves, chopped finely
1 sprig of rosemary, chopped finely
grated zest and juice of ½ lemon
¼ cup goat's cheese, or 4 tablespoons soy cream
sea salt and black pepper to taste
flat leaf parsley or grated Parmesan to garnish

In a large saucepan, heat the oil and cook the shallots, garlic, and celery over medium heat for 4 minutes. Add the rice and stir well. Add 2 ladles of the warmed stock and stir until the rice has absorbed most of the liquid. Keep adding the stock gradually for about 10 more minutes, stirring constantly.

Add the asparagus, herbs, and lemon zest, and continue to cook gently, stirring, for a further 10 minutes. At no point should you allow the mixture to become too dry—add more stock as necessary.

When the rice is cooked, mix in the goat's cheese or soy cream, and lemon juice. Season to taste with salt and pepper, and sprinkle with the parsley or Parmesan just before serving.

TIP
You can add the tough ends of the asparagus spears to your vegetable stock. This will give the risotto more flavor.

PRESERVING HERBS

It is possible to preserve fresh herbs by drying or freezing them. The herbs most suited to drying are marjoram, oregano, mint, rosemary, and thyme. Just tie the stalks in bunches and hang them upside down in a warm airy place until they are dry, or spread the sprigs out on racks or trays, cover with a fine cloth such as muslin, and leave them in a warm, airy room for about 24 hours. Another option is freezing—herbs such as basil, chervil, dill, tarragon, and parsley are the most successful. Simply pack the leaves or sprigs in small plastic freezer bags or add chopped herbs to water and freeze them in ice trays. Freezing actually retains the fresh flavor far better than drying, so it is a good habit to adopt—especially as fresh herbs bought in supermarkets can be quite costly.

Asparagus and Lemon Risotto

International Pizzas

The first pizzas were made in Naples in the early 1800s, but flat bread made from wheat-based yeast dough had been made there for centuries. Today it is enjoyed all over the world, and different variations have been created to suit the local specialties.

A real Italian pizza is baked in a wood-fired brick oven so hot that it is cooked in only a few minutes. However, with pizza stones and a hot oven, you can also achieve excellent results at home. Use a slab of unglazed terracotta from a tile center and it will cost you a fraction of the price of the pizza stones you find in specialist kitchenware shops.

Preparation time:
45 minutes
(plus 1–2 hours)

Cooking time:
15–20 minutes

Basic Pizza Dough V

MAKES 4 X 9-INCH OR 2 X 12-INCH PIZZA BASES

1 cup water (½ cup boiling to ½ cup cold)
2 teaspoons dried yeast
2 tablespoons extra virgin olive oil
1 teaspoon superfine sugar
1 pound all-purpose flour
pinch of sea salt

Mix the water, yeast, oil, and sugar together in a small bowl, and leave it for a few minutes. Sift the flour and salt into a large bowl and make a well in the center. Stir in the yeast mixture to form a dough. Turn it out onto a floured surface and knead it firmly for at least 10 minutes until it becomes elastic. Place it in a large, greased bowl and cover with a damp tea towel or plate. Leave it to rise for about 1–2 hours, until it has doubled in size.

Turn it out onto a floured surface and punch it down. Cut it into four pieces of equal size and roll these into balls (you can refrigerate or freeze the dough at this stage). Take one ball at a time and, using a rolling pin, roll it out until it is thin and about 9 inches in diameter. Arrange the topping of your choice on the base, lift it carefully onto an oiled and preheated baking sheet or pizza stone. Bake in a preheated oven at 450°F for 15–20 minutes, until the outside edge is golden and the topping is cooked through.

TIP
Try adding fresh herbs, sun-dried tomatoes, chopped chili peppers, etc. to the pizza base before cooking it.

English Breakfast Pizza ~ *UK*

FOR 1 X 12-INCH PIZZA BASE (SEE BASIC RECIPE ON PAGE 116)

Preparation time: **20 minutes**

Cooking time: **15–20 minutes**

3 tablespoons tomato purée
2–3 vegetarian sausages, lightly browned and cut in half across
4 slices vegetarian bacon slices, sautéed lightly
2 tomatoes, sliced thickly
2 medium mushrooms, sliced
sea salt and black pepper to taste
olive oil
¼ pound vegetarian mozzarella, sliced
1 poached organic egg per person (optional)

Spread the tomato purée over the pizza base. Arrange the prepared sausages, bacon, tomatoes, and mushrooms on top. Season to taste with salt and pepper, drizzle with a little olive oil, and cover with the sliced mozzarella.

Bake at 450°F for 15–20 minutes until the base is crisp and the topping is lightly browned.

If you are using them, have the freshly poached eggs ready by the end of the cooking time, slip them on top, and serve at once.

California Vegetable Pizza ~ *USA*

(See photograph on pages 116–7)

FOR 1 X 12-INCH PIZZA BASE (SEE BASIC RECIPE ON PAGE 116)

Preparation time: **15–20 minutes**

Cooking time: **15–20 minutes**

3 tablespoons Salsa (page 151)
8–10 spinach leaves, sautéed briefly in a little oil
6–8 baby corn
10 snow peas, blanched briefly and sliced in half
½ yellow bell pepper, seeded, roasted, peeled, and sliced
½ ripe avocado, sliced
5 cherry tomatoes, cut in half
sea salt and black pepper to taste
¼ pound vegetarian mozzarella, sliced
1 tablespoon olive oil
freshly chopped or dried marjoram or oregano

Spread the pizza base with the salsa. Arrange the prepared vegetables decoratively on top and season to taste with salt and pepper. Cover with the sliced mozzarella and brush the rim of the pizza with olive oil.

Bake at 450°F for 15–20 minutes until the base is crisp and the topping is lightly browned.

Siam Pizza ~ *Thailand*

Preparation time: **10–15 minutes**

Cooking time: **15–20 minutes**

FOR 1 X 12-INCH PIZZA BASE (SEE BASIC RECIPE ON PAGE 116)

3 tablespoons Satay Sauce (page 148)
1/3 cup carrots, coarsely grated
3–4 scallions, chopped
1/4 cup marinated tofu (page 74)
soy sauce to taste
1–2 tablespoons olive oil
2 tablespoons freshly chopped coriander (or flat leaf parsley if preferred)
a little finely chopped chili pepper to taste (optional)
2 teaspoons sesame seeds
1/4 pound vegetarian mozzarella, sliced

Spread the pizza base with the satay sauce, then the carrots, and sprinkle with the scallions. Arrange the tofu on top, drizzle with a little soy sauce to taste and a little of the olive oil. Sprinkle with the chopped coriander or parsley, then the optional chili pepper and sesame seeds. Cover with the sliced mozzarella. Brush the rim of the pizza with the rest of the oil.

Bake at 450°F for 15–20 minutes until the base is crisp and the topping is lightly browned.

Athenian Pizza ~ *Greece*

Preparation time: **15 minutes**

Cooking time: **15–20 minutes**

FOR 1 X 12-INCH PIZZA BASE (SEE BASIC RECIPE ON PAGE 116)

2 tablespoons extra virgin olive oil
1 small red onion, sliced
3/4 cup mushrooms, sliced
10 black olives, pitted
3 tablespoons peperoncini (pickled mild peppers), sliced
1/4 cup vegetarian feta
1 tablespoon freshly chopped oregano or basil
sea salt and black pepper to taste
fresh oregano sprigs or basil leaves to garnish

Spread the pizza base with some of the olive oil. Arrange the onion, mushrooms, olives, and peperoncini on the base. Crumble the feta on top, and sprinkle with the oregano or basil. Season liberally and drizzle with the rest of the olive oil.

Bake at 450°F for 15–20 minutes until the base is crisp and the topping is lightly browned. Garnish with a sprig or two of fresh oregano or basil leaves.

Preparation time:
30 minutes

Cooking time:
40 minutes

GREAT PIZZA TOPPINGS

* Roasted red onion with vegetarian Gorgonzola, and rosemary (see photograph on page 117)
* Arugula, artichokes, olives, vegetarian mozzarella and Parmesan
* Roasted garlic, sun-dried tomatoes, herbs, and vegetarian feta
* Roasted potato, garlic, cooked leeks, fresh thyme, and vegetarian mozzarella
* Sliced roasted red pepper, sautéed with finely sliced leek and topped with vegetarian pecorino
* Caramelized Onions (page 131), capers, roasted eggplant with balsamic vinegar, Pesto Sauce (page 148), vegetarian mozzarella and Parmesan
* Eggplant cooked in Szechuan Sauce (page 18), chopped red onion, and vegetarian mozzarella
* Fresh spinach leaves with garlic, pine nuts, raisins, and vegetarian Fontina
* Pickled jalapeños, coriander, Salsa (page 151), pinto beans, mashed avocado or guacamole, sour cream, and mature vegetarian Cheddar or Monteray Jack cheese
* Stir-fried Snow Peas with Ginger and Garlic (page 126), tofu pieces, and corn

BUILD YOUR OWN PIZZA PARTY

Have a pile of freshly baked pizza bases and invite your guests to show their originality by mixing their own ingredients for toppings. Lay out a buffet table with the ingredients below, and make a large tossed salad to go with the pizzas. A good rustic red wine and a couple of your favorite desserts will make a perfect feast.

* sliced fresh tomatoes
* sliced bell peppers, all colors
* thinly sliced red onion
* chopped scallions
* coarsely chopped garlic cloves
* assorted pitted olives
* Pesto Sauce (page 148)
* sun-dried tomatoes
* arugula
* pineapple rings
* capers
* quartered canned artichoke hearts
* sautéed or grilled eggplant slices
* assorted vegetarian cheeses, grated and sliced, e.g. mozzarella, Cheddar, Fontina, Gouda, or Gorgonzola
* tomato sauce or Salsa (page 151)
* grated vegetarian Parmesan
* bowls of olive oil, with brushes
* a big bowl of freshly chopped herbs
* sea salt and black pepper

Tuscan Beans with Tomatoes, Garlic, and Sage Ⓥ *Italy*

Preparation time:
30–40 minutes

This rich bean dish is dominated by the delicious flavor of sage and garlic. Serve with a crisp green salad.

SERVES 4

1 medium onion, chopped
3 cloves garlic, chopped
3 tablespoons olive oil
1¼ cups canned haricot (navy), cannellini (white kidney), or butter (lima) beans
⅔ pound spinach, washed and dried
2 large ripe tomatoes, skinned and chopped (see tip)
2 tablespoons freshly chopped sage
sea salt and black pepper to taste
1¼ cups vegetable stock (page 32)
4 rounds of ciabatta bread, toasted

In a large saucepan, sauté the onion and garlic in the oil until softened slightly, about 3–4 minutes. Add the drained beans, spinach, tomatoes, and sage to the pan. Add ⅔ cup of stock. Cover and simmer over very low heat for about 15 minutes, topping up with stock as necessary. Season to taste with salt and pepper. Put a round of toasted bread into each serving bowl and ladle some of the beans on top.

SKINNING TOMATOES
Put the tomatoes in a large bowl, cover with boiling water, and leave for about 30 seconds. Lift them out one by one and pierce the skin with a sharp knife; it will peel off easily.

Artichoke Casserole with Pine Nuts ~ *Spain*

Preparation time
50 minutes

This rich, peasant-style casserole is particularly good served with a crusty loaf of bread to soak up the juices.

SERVES 4

3 tablespoons olive oil
4 vegetarian bacon slices, cut into strips
1 large onion, chopped
3 cloves garlic, chopped
1 pound ripe plum tomatoes, skinned and chopped (see tip)
2 cups vegetable stock (page 32)
2 x 14-ounce cans of artichoke hearts, drained and halved
sea salt and black pepper to taste
3 tablespoons pine nuts, toasted (page 70)

In a small frying pan, heat 1 tablespoon of the oil and cook the bacon over medium heat until it is lightly browned. Remove it from the pan and set it aside.

Heat the remaining oil in a large saucepan and soften the onion and garlic over low heat for 5–7 minutes. Stir in the prepared tomatoes and cook uncovered for 10 minutes or until the tomatoes are reduced to a sauce consistency. Add the stock and season to taste with salt and pepper. Bring to a boil, add the artichokes, cover, and simmer for 12–15 minutes.

Turn the casserole out into a serving dish and sprinkle with the cooked bacon pieces and pine nuts. Serve immediately.

Eggplant, Sweet Potato, and Goat's Cheese Gratin ~ *UK*

Preparation time:
40 minutes

Cooking time:
30 minutes

This was created by my friend Joanne. It is an unusual combination that really works. Everyone who has it thinks it is wonderful.

SERVES 6

2 medium eggplants, sliced diagonally ½ inch thick
4 tablespoons olive oil
5 cloves garlic, sliced in half lengthwise
sea salt and black pepper to taste
2 tablespoons balsamic vinegar
6 medium sweet potatoes, peeled and sliced ½ inch thick
3 tablespoons vegetarian Parmesan, grated
¾ cup vegetarian Cheddar, grated
handful of fresh basil leaves
½ pound vegetarian goat's cheese, sliced
Roasted Red Pepper Sauce (page 149)

Lay the eggplant slices on a baking sheet and brush them with olive oil. Turn them over, scatter the garlic slices over them and brush with a little more oil. Season to taste with salt and pepper and bake at 425°F. Turn when lightly browned, after about 10 minutes, bake for another 10 minutes, then remove from the oven. Drizzle with balsamic vinegar and let them cool.

In a large saucepan, blanch the sweet potato slices in boiling water for 3–4 minutes. Drain and cool.

Layer half of the sweet potatoes in a large baking dish. Sprinkle with one-third of the Parmesan and Cheddar, and season to taste with salt and pepper. Arrange half of the basil leaves evenly on top. Lay half of the eggplant slices over the basil and distribute the halved garlic cloves evenly. Place half of the goat's cheese slices on top. Repeat the layers and sprinkle with the remaining third of the Parmesan and Cheddar. Bake at 400°F for 30 minutes until lightly browned on top.

Butternut Squash Pilaf (V) *Morocco*

Preparation time: *30 minutes*

Cooking time: *20–30 minutes*

This dish is typical of North Africa where sugar and sweet spices are often used in savory recipes.

SERVES 4

1 large onion, chopped
½–⅔ cup butter or margarine
1 cup long-grain rice
1 red chili pepper, seeded and chopped
3 whole cloves
2 tablespoons sultanas
2½ cups water
sea salt and black pepper to taste
1 butternut squash, weighing about 1½ pounds, peeled and cubed
4 tablespoons raw sugar
2 teaspoons ground cinnamon
1 teaspoon ground allspice

In a large saucepan, sauté the onion in 4 tablespoons of butter or margarine for about 5 minutes until softened. Add the rice, chili pepper, cloves, and sultanas, and stir thoroughly. Add the water and bring to a boil. Reduce the heat, cover, and simmer for about 15 minutes until the water has been absorbed. Season to taste with salt and pepper.

Steam the squash for about 5 minutes until just tender. Butter a large ovenproof dish and sprinkle the base with 1 tablespoon of sugar. Mix the remaining sugar with the spices. Melt the remaining butter or margarine.

Arrange half of squash in the dish, sprinkle with half of the spice mixture, and drizzle with half of the remaining butter or margarine. Spoon the rice on top, then repeat the layer once more, finishing with the butter or margarine.

Bake in the oven at 400°F for 20–30 minutes until lightly caramelized on the surface.

Serve at once with sautéed mushrooms, or grilled eggplant slices, and some warmed pita bread.

CHILI PEPPERS

Chili peppers come in many varieties. The plump red or green jalapeño pepper is perhaps the best known hot type, and is often used in Mexican cooking. Anaheims can also be red or green, and are about 4 inches long with a blunt end, but can be quite mild—a good choice for the timid. Thai or birdseye chilies are the tiniest of all, but don't be fooled—they are extremely hot! They can be green, white, orange, and red, and are sharpely pointed and very pretty. Whichever chili pepper you choose, always remove the seeds and veins first. I keep a store of dried red chilies (often Poblanos) in the cupboard, but they can be very hot. Canned peppers tend to be milder and are a truly delicious way of spicing up dishes, but beware of chilies in vinegar—they can blow your head off!

Mushroom Roast ~ *UK*

This recipe was suggested by my friend Julia. It is a great centerpiece for a vegetarian Christmas. It is delicious served hot with Onion and Juniper Gravy (page 151) or cold with a salad.

Preparation time:
30 minutes

Cooking time:
40–45 minutes

SERVES 4–6

1 medium onion, chopped
2 tablespoons olive oil
½ each green, red and yellow bell pepper, seeded and chopped
1 pound brown mushrooms, sliced
3 cups brown breadcrumbs
1 tablespoon dried mixed herbs, or 2 tablespoons fresh herbs of your choice
1 large organic egg, beaten
sea salt and black pepper to taste
paprika to taste
1 cup vegetarian Cheddar, grated
1 large or 2 small tomatoes, sliced

In a large saucepan, sauté the onion in the oil for 5 minutes. Stir in the chopped peppers and cook for a further 5 minutes, stirring occasionally.

Add the sliced mushrooms and cook gently until they soften for 1 or 2 minutes. Remove from the heat, stir in the breadcrumbs and herbs, and mix well. Fold in the beaten egg. Season with salt and pepper and a little paprika to taste.

Spoon the mixture into a well-greased 9 x 5 x 3-inch loaf pan and press down well. Sprinkle the grated cheese on top and bake at 350°F for 40–45 minutes. Arrange the tomato slices on top for the last 15 minutes of baking.

Allow the roast to cook for at least 20 minutes before lifting it out carefully, then slice it with a very sharp knife.

Side Dishes

Chargrilled Vegetables (V) *Spain*

SERVES 4

Preparation time: 30–40 minutes

1 medium eggplant
2 medium zucchini
1 yellow bell pepper, seeded and quartered
2 medium potatoes, washed, cut into chunks, and blanched
4–6 tablespoons olive oil
4 large flat mushrooms, sliced
2 medium tomatoes, quartered
sea salt and black pepper to taste
Classic Vinaigrette (page 151), made with garlic
freshly chopped coriander (or flat leaf parsley if preferred) to garnish

Cut the eggplant and zucchini into chunky sticks. Grill and skin the pepper.

Put the eggplant, zucchini, yellow pepper, and potatoes in a large bowl and drizzle a little oil over them and toss, then repeat until they are well covered.

Preheat the broiler to maximum temperature. Put the vegetables in a roasting pan in a single layer. Grill and turn until they brown nicely all over.

Remove the roasting pan, add the mushrooms and tomatoes, and toss well. Return the pan to the broiler for a further 10 minutes or until the vegetables are tender and well grilled. Put them on a plate to cool.

When the vegetables have cooled, season to taste with salt and pepper, toss them in sufficient garlic vinaigrette to moisten them, and serve at room temperature, sprinkled with a little chopped coriander or parsley.

Snow Peas with Ginger and Garlic (V) *China*

SERVES 2–3

Preparation time: 15 minutes

1 teaspoon cornstarch
5 tablespoons vegetable stock (page 32)
3 tablespoons butter or margarine
2 cloves garlic, chopped finely
2 thin slices fresh ginger, shredded finely
½ pound snow peas, trimmed
sea salt and black pepper to taste
1 tablespoon soy sauce
sesame seeds, toasted (page 60)

Mix the cornstarch into the stock. In a large frying pan, melt the butter or margarine and add the garlic and ginger. Stir-fry for 1 minute over medium heat.

Add the snow peas and coat well with the butter or margarine. Season to taste with salt and pepper, add the stock mixture and soy sauce, and cook for 2–3 minutes, until the snow peas turn bright green. Serve garnished with sesame seeds.

Chilli Spring Greens

Chili Spring Greens V *Kenya*

Preparation time: 25 minutes

SERVES 4–6

2 pounds kale or spring greens, washed and chopped
4 tablespoons water or vegetable stock (page 32)
2 tablespoons peanut oil
1 medium onion, chopped finely
1 medium tomato, skinned and chopped finely
1 chili pepper, seeded and chopped finely
sea salt and black pepper to taste
4 tablespoons ground peanuts
2 teaspoons fresh lemon juice

Put the chopped greens in a large saucepan with the water or stock and cook gently, covered, for 10 minutes, until tender.

Meanwhile, in a medium frying pan, heat the peanut oil and sauté the chopped onion, tomato, and chili pepper for 2–3 minutes.

Place the sautéed onion mixture on the greens, but do not stir it in. Season to taste with salt and pepper. Sprinkle the ground peanuts on top. Cover and steam gently for a further 10 minutes.

Add the lemon juice, check the seasoning, and serve.

Oven Fries V *UK*

SERVES 3–4

Preparation time: ***10 minutes***

Cooking time: ***20–25 minutes***

1 pound potatoes, cut into medium fries
3 tablespoons olive oil
1 tablespoon soy sauce
garlic powder (optional)
sea salt and black pepper to taste

In a large bowl, toss the potatoes in the oil and soy sauce, and sprinkle them with garlic powder.

Transfer the fries to a baking sheet and roast at 425°F for 25–30 minutes, turning them from time to time until they turn golden brown. Sprinkle the fries with salt and pepper to taste, and serve at once.

Yam Fries V *USA*

SERVES 3–4

Preparation time: ***20 minutes***

1 pound yams, peeled
chili powder or cayenne pepper
oil for deep frying
sea salt to taste

Cut the yams into slices and then into fries. Put them in a medium saucepan, cover with cold water, and bring to a boil. Cook for 5 minutes, then drain and dry the fries on paper towels. Sprinkle with a good pinch of chili powder or cayenne pepper.

Pour 2–3 inches of oil into a medium saucepan and place over medium to high heat. The oil is ready when a cube of bread browns immediately. Cook the fries for 6–8 minutes until they are golden and crisp. Drain them on paper towels, sprinkle with salt to taste, and serve at once.

Marinated Tofu Fries V *China*

SERVES 4

Preparation time: ***20 minutes (plus marinating time)***

1 pound firm tofu, cut into ½-inch batons
5 tablespoons water
2 cloves garlic
⅔ cup red wine vinegar
dash of red wine (optional)
⅔ cup soy sauce or tamari
3 cloves
2 tablespoons sugar
sea salt and black pepper to taste
peanut oil for deep frying

Drain the tofu for 10 minutes on a clean tea towel to remove the excess moisture.

Combine the remaining ingredients in a small saucepan and simmer slowly for 5–10 minutes. Place the tofu in a bowl, pour the marinade over it, and leave it in a cool place for a minimum of 1 hour or refrigerate for up to 24 hours.

Pour 2–3 inches of oil into a medium saucepan and place over medium to high heat. The oil is ready when a cube of bread browns immediately. Carefully lower the drained tofu into the oil, a batch at a time, and fry until it turns golden brown all over. Drain on paper towels, and serve at once.

Potato and Onion Gratin **V** *France*

Preparation time: *20 minutes*

Cooking time: *1 hour 30 minutes*

SERVES 4

1 pound waxy potatoes, peeled and sliced thinly
2 cups onions, sliced thinly
1 clove garlic, halved
sea salt and black pepper to taste
3 cups dairy or soy milk, or light dairy or soy cream
3 tablespoons butter or margarine

Rinse the potatoes in cold water to wash out some of the starch, and dry them thoroughly. Rub a deep earthenware dish with a cut clove of garlic. Arrange alternate layers of potato and onion in the dish, seasoning generously between each layer.

Pour the milk or cream over the potatoes, and dot the top with little pieces of butter or margarine. Bake at 325°F for 1½ hours, turning the heat up to 400°F for the last 10 minutes to brown and crisp the top.

Special Mashed Potatoes **V** *UK*

Preparation time: *30 minutes*

SERVES 4

5 medium floury potatoes, peeled and quartered
2 tablespoons dairy or soy milk, or dairy or soy cream
1 tablespoon butter or margarine
1 tablespoon finely chopped scallion
2 teaspoons freshly chopped herb of your choice
sea salt and black pepper to taste

In a medium saucepan, boil the potatoes in lightly salted water for about 20 minutes until tender, then drain.

Add the milk or cream and butter or margarine, mash the potatoes, then whisk them with a fork until they are creamy, fluffy, and lump-free.

Fold in the scallion and herbs, and season to taste with salt and pepper.

Potatoes with Lemon **V** *Greece*

Preparation time: *15 minutes*

Cooking time: *1 hour*

SERVES 4

2 pounds medium potatoes, peeled
juice of 1 lemon
sea salt and black pepper to taste
6 tablespoons (¾ stick) butter or margarine
⅔ cup hot water

Halve the potatoes lengthwise, then quarter them to make wedges. Arrange them in a medium ovenproof dish and pour the lemon juice over them. Season to taste with salt and pepper, and dot with the butter or margarine.

Pour the water into the dish and bake uncovered at 375°F for about 1 hour until tender, basting at least twice while the potatoes are cooking.

Herby Potato Cakes (V) *UK*

SERVES 4–6

Preparation time: 45 minutes

2 pounds potatoes, peeled and cubed
4 tablespoons (1/2 stick) butter or margarine
2 tablespoons freshly chopped mixed herbs, e.g. parsley, chives, sage, thyme, rosemary, marjoram, or 1 tablespoon mixed dried herbs
sea salt and black pepper to taste
freshly grated nutmeg
2 tablespoons dairy or soy cream
vegetable oil for shallow frying

In a medium saucepan, cook the potatoes in boiling water for 15 minutes or until they are tender. Drain. Melt the butter or margarine in the same pan and mix in the herbs. Cook very gently for 2–3 minutes.

Return the potatoes to the pan. Heat gently and mash thoroughly until fluffy. Season well with salt, pepper, and some grated nutmeg, and stir in the cream.

Allow the potatoes to cool before shaping them into thin cakes with floured hands. Heat 1/4 inch of oil in a large frying pan until it is hot. Fry the cakes until they are golden brown on each side. Serve at once.

Potato Fry (V) *India*

SERVES 4

Preparation time: 40–50 minutes

3 large potatoes, peeled
1 teaspoon chili powder
4 tablespoons freshly chopped coriander (or flat leaf parsley if preferred)
sea salt and black pepper to taste
4–6 tablespoons vegetable oil for frying

Grate the potatoes and soak them in cold water for 10 minutes before draining and drying them thoroughly on a clean tea towel. Put them in a medium bowl, mix the potatoes with the chili powder and coriander or parsley, and season to taste with salt and pepper.

Heat 2–3 tablespoons of the oil in a large frying pan and spread the potato mixture over it. Press it down to form a thick pancake and fry over medium heat until the base is browned and crisp, about 10–15 minutes.

Turn the potato fry over carefully, add 2–3 tablespoons of oil to the pan, and cook the other side until it is crisp and golden, for 10–15 minutes. Serve in wedges.

TIP
An easy way to flip the potato fry is to turn it out, upside down, onto a plate the same size as the frying pan, then add a little fresh oil to the pan and slide it off the plate and back into the pan.

Candied Sweet Potatoes ♥ *Caribbean*

Preparation time:
10 minutes

Cooking time:
40–45 minutes

SERVES 6

2 pounds sweet potatoes, washed and sliced
3/4 cup dark brown sugar
grated zest of 1/2 lemon
4 tablespoons (1/2 stick) butter or margarine, melted

Mix all the ingredients together in a greased, medium ovenproof dish. Cover with foil and bake at 400°F for 40–45 minutes, until the sweet potatoes are tender.

Hawaiian-style Sweet Potatoes ♥ *Hawaii*

Preparation time:
45 minutes

Cooking time:
20 minutes

SERVES 3–4

1 pound sweet potatoes, washed
1 banana, peeled and cubed
2 tablespoons brown sugar
juice of 1/2 grapefruit
2 tablespoons dried coconut

In a medium saucepan, boil the sweet potatoes in their skins for 30–35 minutes, until tender. Allow them to cool, then peel and cube them. Mix with the banana, and spoon into a medium casserole dish.

In a small saucepan, dissolve the sugar in the grapefruit juice over gentle heat, and pour it over the sweet potato and banana. Bake at 375°F for 20 minutes.

Sprinkle the coconut on top and place the dish under a preheated broiler for 1 minute until it is lightly browned.

Caramelized Onions ♥ *France*

Preparation time:
1 hour

SERVES 4

2 tablespoons (1/4 stick) butter or margarine
2 pounds white and red onions, sliced
3 tablespoons sugar
sea salt and black pepper to taste
a little cold water

In a large saucepan, melt the butter or margarine and toss the onion slices in it until they are evenly coated. Sprinkle the sugar over the onions, season to taste with salt and pepper, and barely cover with cold water.

Bring to a boil and simmer, uncovered, until the water evaporates—30–40 minutes. Stir the onions towards the end of the cooking time to prevent them from burning. Serve warm.

Green Beans with Almonds V *France*

SERVES 2–3

Preparation time: 10–15 minutes

½ pound thin green beans
2 tablespoons flaked almonds, toasted (page 70)
2–3 tablespoons freshly chopped dill
1 teaspoon olive oil
sea salt and black pepper to taste

Steam the beans for 4–5 minutes until *al dente*. Stir in the remaining ingredients, and serve.

Grilled Zucchini with Red Sauce V *Italy*

SERVES 2–3

Preparation time: 15 minutes

3 tablespoons olive oil
2 medium zucchini, cut into ½-inch slices
2 large tomatoes, seeded and diced
3 cloves garlic, thinly sliced
1 red bell pepper, roasted, skinned, and diced
sea salt and black pepper to taste

Put 2 tablespoons of the oil in a medium bowl and add the zucchini slices. Toss them with your hands to coat them thoroughly with oil.

Grill the zucchini on a preheated griddle or under the broiler until lightly charred, 4 minutes on each side.

Heat the remaining oil in a small frying pan. When it is hot, carefully add the tomatoes and garlic. When the garlic starts to color, add the red pepper. Spoon the tomato mixture over the zucchini and season to taste with salt and pepper.

Button Onions with Cream and Thyme V *Spain*

SERVES 4

Preparation time: 40–45 minutes

1½ pounds button onions
2 tablespoons (¼ stick) butter or margarine
1 tablespoon freshly chopped thyme
1½ cups vegetable stock (page 32)
½ cup dairy or warmed soy cream
sea salt and black pepper to taste

To peel the onions, submerge them in a bowl of boiling water for 5 minutes, drain, and allow them to cool slightly before making a cut in the bottom of each one with a sharp knife. The onions will then pop out of their skins easily.

In a medium frying pan, melt the butter or margarine and sauté the onions, shaking the pan occasionally, for 8–10 minutes until they start to brown. Add the thyme and stock, and bring to a boil. Then reduce the heat and simmer, uncovered, for 15 minutes or until the onions are cooked but still slightly crisp.

Pour in the cream and heat through. Check the seasoning and serve.

Top to bottom: Green Beans with Almonds, Grilled Zucchini with Red Sauce, Button Onions with Cream and Thyme

Grilled Squash with Herb Butter V *USA*

SERVES 4–6

Preparation time: ***30–40 minutes***

1½ pounds squash, peeled and seeded
2 tablespoons olive oil
sea salt and black pepper to taste
8 tablespoons (1 stick) butter or margarine, melted
1 shallot, chopped finely
1 medium clove garlic, crushed
2 teaspoons fresh lemon juice
¼ teaspoon finely grated lemon zest
2 tablespoons freshly chopped parsley
2 teaspoons freshly chopped thyme
2 teaspoons freshly chopped marjoram

Cut the squash into ½-inch slices. Brush the slices with olive oil and season to taste with salt and pepper. Grill the squash—preferably on a charcoal grill—for 5–6 minutes on each side until tender.

Meanwhile, make the herb butter by combining the remaining ingredients in a small saucepan and heating them gently. Drizzle the herb butter over the squash and serve.

Winter Squash Baked with Leeks V *USA*

SERVES 4

Preparation time: ***25 minutes***

Cooking time: ***20 minutes***

1 pound squash, peeled, seeded, and cubed
1 pound leeks, washed, trimmed, and chopped roughly
2 cloves garlic, chopped finely
4 tablespoons olive oil
sea salt and black pepper to taste
8–12 fresh sage leaves

In a large saucepan, toss the squash, leeks, garlic, and olive oil over medium heat for 5–6 minutes. Season to taste with salt and pepper.

Put the vegetables in a medium baking dish and add the sage leaves. Cover with foil and bake at 425°F for about 20 minutes, until the vegetables are tender.

Spicy Okra V *India*

SERVES 4

Preparation time: ***15 minutes***

1¼ cups coconut milk
¾ pound okra, trimmed
2 tablespoons vegetable oil
2 small dried chili peppers, left whole
1 clove garlic, crushed
1 teaspoon each cumin seeds, mustard seeds, and poppy seeds
fresh lemon juice to taste

In a medium saucepan, heat the coconut milk gently and simmer the okra in it until tender, about 7–8 minutes.

Heat the oil in a small frying pan and brown the chili peppers, garlic, and spices until the seeds begin to spit. Remove the whole chili peppers and pour the spicy oil over the okra. Add a squeeze of lemon juice. Serve hot or cold.

Summer Squash with Dill and Sour Cream ~ *Hungary*

Preparation time:
40 minutes

SERVES 4

1½ pounds summer squash, peeled, seeded, and grated
sea salt
2 tablespoons (¼ stick) butter or margarine
1 small onion, chopped
2 tablespoons all-purpose flour
2 tablespoons freshly chopped dill
¾ cup vegetable stock (page 32)
⅔ cup sour cream
2 teaspoons white wine vinegar
1 teaspoon superfine sugar

Put the grated summer squash in a colander and sprinkle lightly with salt. Let it sit for 30 minutes.

In a large saucepan, melt the butter or margarine and add the onion. Cover the pan and cook the onion over gentle heat until it is soft and translucent, for about 5–6 minutes, stirring occasionally.

Sprinkle the flour over the onion and stir well. Add the dill and mix again, then stir in the stock. Simmer and stir until the sauce thickens, for about 3–4 minutes.

Squeeze the excess moisture from the squash before adding it to the sauce. Stir in the sour cream, then the vinegar and sugar, and cook for 5 minutes before serving.

Roasted Mushrooms with Peperonata V *Italy*

Preparation time:
45 minutes
Cooking time:
15 minutes

SERVES 6

1½ pounds mushrooms, sliced thickly
½ cup olive oil
2 large white onions, sliced finely
2 cloves garlic, crushed
1 bay leaf
3 each red and yellow bell peppers, seeded, and cut into strips
14-ounce can chopped tomatoes, drained
sea salt and black pepper to taste
4 tablespoons red wine vinegar
2 tablespoons freshly chopped basil

Arrange the mushrooms on a baking sheet and drizzle liberally with half of the olive oil. Roast at 400°F for 15 minutes.

In a large saucepan, heat the remaining oil and sauté the onions until they are golden and translucent, for about 10 minutes. Add the garlic and bay leaf, and continue to cook for 3 minutes. Add the peppers and cook for a further 10–15 minutes, stirring continuously until just tender. Then add the tomatoes and season to taste with salt and pepper. Simmer uncovered for 10 minutes until the juices from the tomatoes have evaporated.

Remove the bay leaf and stir in the vinegar and basil. Let the sauce cool, then stir in the mushrooms and serve.

Glazed Carrots with Honey and Sesame Seeds V *USA*

Preparation time: 15–20 minutes

SERVES 4

1 pound carrots, peeled
4 tablespoons (1/2 stick) butter or margarine
2 tablespoons honey (or maple syrup for vegans)
pinch of sea salt
1 1/4 cups water
1 tablespoon sesame seeds, toasted (page 60)

Cut the carrots into sticks and put them in a medium pan with half of the butter or margarine, honey or maple syrup, and a pinch of salt, then add the water. Bring to a boil, uncovered, and cook rapidly until the water has all but evaporated and the carrots are tender, for about 8 minutes.

Add the remaining butter or margarine and honey or maple syrup and cook until a thick syrup forms to coat the carrots, for 3–4 minutes longer. Serve sprinkled with the sesame seeds.

Spicy Corn V *Mexico*

Preparation time: 20 minutes

SERVES 2–3

1 tablespoon olive oil
1 red bell pepper, diced
2 teaspoons mild chili powder
1 1/2 cups corn kernels
4 scallions, chopped finely
2–3 tablespoons freshly chopped coriander (or flat leaf parsley if preferred)
juice of 1 lime
sea salt and black pepper to taste

In a medium frying pan, heat the oil and add the red pepper and chili powder. When the oil sizzles, add the corn and cook for 5 minutes. Add the remaining ingredients and season to taste with salt and pepper.

Oven-roasted Vegetable Fries with Whole Garlic V *USA*

Preparation time: 15–20 minutes

Cooking time: 20–25 minutes

SERVES 3–4

1 large parsnip
1 large turnip
1 large beet
1 small fennel bulb
1 medium celery root, peeled
3–4 tablespoons olive oil
12–16 cloves garlic, unpeeled
sea salt and black pepper to taste

Scrub the root vegetables thoroughly but leave them unpeeled. Cut them into fries and transfer them to a large bowl. Toss them with the olive oil and garlic until they are well coated. Season with salt and pepper.

Spread the vegetables evenly on a baking sheet in a single layer. Roast at 425°F for 20–25 minutes until they are crisp and tender, turning them from time to time so that they brown all over. Serve hot.

Top to bottom: Glazed Carrots with Honey and Sesame Seeds, Spicy Corn, Oven-roasted Vegetable Fries with Whole Garlic

Red Cabbage with Apple (V) *Russia*

SERVES 4–6

Preparation time: ***1 hour 20 minutes***

2 tablespoons (1/4 stick) butter or margarine
1 medium onion, diced
1 medium red cabbage, core discarded and sliced (about 1 1/4 pounds prepared weight)
1 1/4 cups water
2 tablespoons vinegar
1 tablespoon brown sugar
sea salt and black pepper to taste
2 medium dessert apples, cored, peeled, and chopped

In a large saucepan, melt the butter or margarine and sauté the onion for about 5 minutes. Stir in the sliced cabbage and toss for a further 2 minutes.

Add the water, vinegar, brown sugar, salt and pepper, and apples. Bring the mixture to a boil, reduce the heat, cover, and simmer for 1 hour.

Crispy Fried Seaweed (V) *China*

SERVES 4

Preparation time: ***15 minutes***

1/2 pound spring greens, outer cabbage leaves, or curly kale, rinsed and dried
vegetable oil for deep frying
soy sauce to taste
chili powder (optional)
2 tablespoons sesame seeds, toasted (page 60)

Lay the leaves on top of each other and roll them up tightly. Using a sharp knife, slice the rolls across into very thin strands, then separate the strands.

Heat 2–3 inches of oil in a wok or large saucepan. The oil is ready when a cube of bread browns immediately. Add a small handful of the greens at a time, standing well back because they spit ferociously as they hit the oil. Allow them to fry for about 1 minute until they shrink and darken, but do not let them overcook and burn. Remove the greens with a slotted spoon, and drain thoroughly on paper towels.

Repeat this process until all the greens have been cooked. Season with soy sauce to taste and an optional pinch of chili powder. Serve sprinkled with the sesame seeds.

Minted Peas (V) *UK*

SERVES 4–6

Preparation time: ***25–30 minutes***

8–12 sprigs of fresh mint, leaves removed and chopped, stalks reserved
1 pound fresh or frozen peas
1 tablespoon butter or margarine
sea salt and black pepper to taste

Pour 2 inches of boiling water into a medium saucepan, add the mint stalks, simmer for 5 minutes, then remove them. Add the peas to the water. Cook frozen peas according to the instructions on the package; if you are using fresh peas, cook them until tender, for 8–10 minutes, then drain.

Stir in the mint leaves and butter or margarine, and season to taste.

Rutabaga Mash with Horseradish V *UK*

Preparation time: 30 minutes

SERVES 4

1 pound rutabaga, peeled and cubed
5 scallions, sliced
2 teaspoons grated horseradish
grated zest and juice of ½ lemon
4 tablespoons dairy or soy cream
sea salt and black pepper to taste

In a medium saucepan, boil the rutabaga for about 15 minutes until tender. Drain. Mash it thoroughly with the remaining ingredients and serve.

Cauliflower with Dijon Mustard Sauce V *France*

Preparation time: 20 minutes

SERVES 3–4

¾ pound cauliflower, cut into florets
4 tablespoons (½ stick) butter or margarine
½ cup all-purpose flour
3 tablespoons Dijon mustard
2½ cups dairy or soy milk
sea salt and black pepper to taste

Steam or boil the cauliflower until tender, for about 5 minutes.

Meanwhile, melt the butter or margarine in a small saucepan, add the flour, and combine thoroughly. Cook gently for 1 minute, stirring. Add the mustard and stir until it is mixed thorough, then gradually pour in the milk, whisking continuously until it thickens and forms a smooth sauce. Bring to a boil and simmer gently for 4–5 minutes.

Put the cauliflower in a medium ovenproof dish, pour the sauce on top, and put the dish under a preheated broiler for 5 minutes until the top turns lightly golden.

Leeks with Balsamic Dressing V *Italy*

Preparation time: 25–30 minutes

SERVES 4

8 small leeks, halved
4 tablespoons olive oil
1 tablespoon balsamic vinegar
1 teaspoon wholegrain mustard
sea salt and black pepper to taste

Steam or boil the leeks until tender, for about 8–10 minutes. Drain thoroughly.

Whisk together the oil, vinegar, and mustard, and season to taste.

Serve the leeks drizzled with the balsamic dressing.

Lemon Spinach ⓥ *Spain*

SERVES 2–3

Preparation time:
10 minutes

1 pound spinach leaves, rinsed
1 teaspoon lemon juice
1 teaspoon grated lemon zest
1/4 teaspoon ground nutmeg
1 tablespoon olive oil
sea salt and black pepper to taste

Put the spinach in a large saucepan and allow it to wilt over high heat for 1–2 minutes. Drain and gently squeeze out the excess water.

Combine the remaining ingredients, toss with the spinach and season to taste with salt and pepper. Serve hot or cold.

Seeded Cabbage ⓥ *Germany*

SERVES 2

Preparation time:
15 minutes

1/2 pound Savoy cabbage, shredded
2 tablespoons (1/4 stick) butter or margarine
1 tablespoon cumin seeds
2 tablespoons mustard seeds
1 teaspoon cider vinegar
sea salt and black pepper to taste

Steam or boil the cabbage until slightly tender, for about 3–4 minutes, then drain. In a large frying pan, heat the butter or margarine and seeds. When the first mustard seeds pop, add the cabbage, vinegar, and seasoning, and cook, stirring, for 5 minutes over medium heat.

Brussels Sprouts with Sesame Seeds ⓥ *UK*

SERVES 3–4

Preparation time:
20 minutes

1 pound Brussels sprouts, trimmed
3 tablespoons sesame oil
2 tablespoons sesame seeds
2 teaspoons paprika
juice of 1/2 lemon or 1 lime
sea salt and black pepper to taste

Put the Brussels sprouts in a medium saucepan. Cover with boiling water and cook until tender, for about 6 minutes, and drain.

Meanwhile, combine the oil, seeds, and paprika in a small saucepan over medium heat. When the seeds begin to color, remove the pan from the heat. Add the lemon or lime juice, season to taste with salt and pepper, and pour the sauce over the Brussels sprouts.

Brussels Sprouts with Chestnuts (V) *UK*

Preparation time: 25 minutes

SERVES 6–8

2 pounds Brussels sprouts, trimmed
4 tablespoons (1/2 stick) butter or margarine
6–8 vegetarian bacon slices, cut into thin strips (optional)
1 cup canned whole chestnuts
sea salt and black pepper to taste

Put the Brussels sprouts in a large saucepan. Cover with boiling water and cook until tender, for about 6 minutes. Drain and return them to the pan.

In a medium frying pan, melt the butter or margarine and fry the bacon pieces until crisp. Stir in the chestnuts and cook for 1–2 minutes until they are warm. Add them to the Brussels spouts, season to taste with salt and pepper, and serve.

Stir-fried Parsnip and Turnip (V) *UK*

Preparation time: 20–25 minutes

SERVES 3–4

2 tablespoons vegetable oil
1/2 pound parsnips, peeled and sliced thinly
1/2 pound turnips, peeled and sliced thinly
1 tablespoon soy sauce
2 cloves garlic, crushed
sea salt and black pepper to taste

Heat the oil in a wok or large frying pan over high heat and toss the vegetables in it for several minutes until they are well coated, beginning to soften, and lightly browned, for about 7–8 minutes.

Add the remaining ingredients, toss well, reduce the heat, and cook for a further 1–2 minutes. Check the seasoning and serve immediately.

Mediterranean-style Green Beans V *Spain*

SERVES 2–3

Preparation time: 6–8 minutes

¾ pound runner or green beans, sliced lengthwise
2 tablespoons freshly chopped basil
1 clove garlic, chopped
sea salt and black pepper to taste
2 tablespoons freshly chopped chives to garnish

Steam or boil the beans until tender, for about 6–8 minutes.

Toss the beans with the basil and garlic, season to taste with salt and pepper, and garnish with chives.

Green Beans with Red Onion V *Belgium*

SERVES 2

Preparation time: 5–6 minutes

½ pound green beans
1 small red onion, finely chopped
2 tablespoons white wine vinegar
1 tablespoon balsamic vinegar
¼ cup olive oil
sea salt and black pepper to taste

Steam or boil the beans until tender, for about 5–6 minutes. Combine the remaining ingredients and pour the sauce over the beans. Season to taste with salt and pepper.

Special Fried Rice V *Thailand*

SERVES 6

Preparation time: 15–20 minutes

1½ cups long-grain rice
2 tablespoons peanut oil
1 medium onion, chopped
1–2 teaspoons soy sauce
2 teaspoons chili bean sauce
3 tablespoons tomato purée
3 tablespoons chopped scallions
2 teaspoons freshly chopped coriander (or flat leaf parsley if preferred)
4 large organic eggs, beaten (optional)

Cook the rice according to the ingredients on the package.

Heat a wok or large frying pan and add the oil. When it is hot, add the chopped onion and stir-fry for 2–3 minutes. Add the rice and continue to toss for 3 minutes.

Add the remaining ingredients, except the eggs, and stir-fry over high heat for 5 minutes. Fold in the beaten eggs, stirring continuously, until they set (omit the eggs for vegans). Serve at once.

Fragrant Coconut Rice V *Thailand*

Preparation time: 30–35 minutes

SERVES 4–6

2 tablespoons peanut oil
1 medium red onion, chopped
2 teaspoons turmeric
1¼ cups long-grain rice
2 cups coconut milk
1¾ cups vegetable stock (page 32)
2 whole cloves
3-inch cinnamon stick
2 bay leaves
⅓ cup broken cashews or toasted almonds (page 70)
soy sauce to taste

Heat the oil in a large saucepan or flameproof casserole dish, add the onion, and stir-fry for 2 minutes.

Add the turmeric and stir for a few moments, then stir in the rice for a further 2–3 minutes. Add the coconut milk and the stock, and bring to a boil. Stir in the cloves, cinnamon, and bay leaves, then reduce the heat as low as possible and cover. Cook undisturbed for 18–20 minutes or until the rice is thoroughly cooked.

Fold in the nuts and add soy sauce to taste. Let the dish sit for 5–10 minutes to allow the flavors to develop.

TIP
Use a heavy-bottomed saucepan because the rice can burn easily.

Fragrant Coconut Rice

Saffron Rice V *India*

SERVES 4

Preparation time: 35–40 minutes

2 tablespoons (1/4 stick) butter or margarine
1 small onion, chopped finely
2 cloves garlic, chopped finely
2 cups vegetable stock (page 32)
large pinch of saffron strands to taste
sea salt and black pepper to taste
3/4 cup basmati rice

In a medium saucepan, heat the butter or margarine, add the onion and garlic, cover, and cook gently until soft and translucent, for about 10 minutes.

Heat the stock, stir in the saffron, and season to taste with salt and pepper.

Toss the rice into the onion mixture and stir for 1–2 minutes. Then add the hot stock and allow the mixture to simmer, covered, for about 15 minutes.

Remove from the heat, season to taste, and leave for 5 minutes before serving to allow the flavors to develop.

Bulgar and Pine Nut Pilaf V *Africa*

SERVES 4

Preparation time: 40–45 minutes

2 tablespoons olive oil
1 small onion, chopped
2 cloves garlic, chopped
1 teaspoon turmeric, or a pinch of saffron strands
1/2 teaspoon ground cinnamon
1 green chili pepper, seeded and chopped
3 cups vegetable stock (page 32)
1 cup bulgar wheat, rinsed under cold water and drained
1 tablespoon butter or margarine
1/2 cup pine nuts
2 tablespoons freshly chopped parsley

In a large saucepan, heat the oil and fry the onion, covered, until tender, for about 8 minutes, stirring occasionally. Add the garlic, turmeric or saffron, cinnamon, and chili pepper, and fry for 1 minute.

Add the stock, bring to a boil, and add the bulgar wheat. Cover and simmer for about 15 minutes, until the stock has absorbed and the bulgar wheat is tender.

Meanwhile, melt the butter or margarine in a small saucepan, add the pine nuts and brown gently, tossing until they are golden all over. Add the pine nuts and parsley to the bulgar wheat, stir with a fork, and serve.

SAFFRON

Saffron used to demand a price higher than gold and is still an expensive spice today. It consists of the stamens of the saffron crocus, which have to be gathered manually and picked out by hand. Over 250,000 flowers must be picked to produce 1 pound of saffron. It is cultivated in many Mediterranean countries, although Spain is the main producer. Some cheaper powdered saffron may be an adulterated form, merely a colored and flavored mixture, so where you can, use the tiny thread-like stamens—they are intensely strong and you need only a pinch to flavor a large quantity of food.

Sauces and Sundries

Sweet and Sour Chili Dipping Sauce V *China*

SERVES 4

Preparation time:
10 minutes

6 tablespoons white or rice vinegar
4 tablespoons brown sugar
1 tablespoon soy sauce
1 small red chili pepper, seeded and chopped very finely
½ teaspoon grated fresh ginger

In a small saucepan, boil the vinegar with the sugar until it has thickened slightly, about 5 minutes. Add the soy sauce and the chili pepper, then stir in the ginger.

Ginger Dipping Sauce V *Vietnam*

SERVES 4

Preparation time:
5 minutes

3 scallions, chopped finely
1 teaspoon grated fresh ginger
1 clove garlic, crushed
2 tablespoons soy sauce
2 tablespoons sesame oil
2 tablespoons cold water

Whisk all the sauce ingredients together in a small bowl.

Chunky Tomato Sauce with Harissa V *North Africa*

SERVES 3–4

Preparation time:
20–25 minutes

2 tablespoons olive oil
1 large onion, chopped finely
14-ounce can chopped tomatoes
1–2 teaspoons harissa paste (see below)

Heat the oil in a medium saucepan. Add the onion, cover, and cook over gentle heat for about 10 minutes until it has softened.

Add the tomatoes with their juices and simmer uncovered for 5 minutes. Stir in the harissa paste and mix well. Taste the sauce and add more harissa if you would like it really spicy. Heat it through just before serving.

HARISSA PASTE

This hot spicy condiment is what gives Moroccan cooking its fiery kick. To make it, you will need 4 tablespoons of dried chili peppers, 2 garlic cloves, a pinch of salt and 2 tablespoons of olive oil. Simply place the chilies in a bowl and pour over enough hot water to cover them. Leave them until the water is cold—at least 2 hours. Drain the chilies and place them in a food processor or blender with the garlic. Process to a thick paste, until the mixture is similar in consistency to tomato purée. Rub the paste through a sieve, being careful not to get any on your hands. Spoon the mixture into a clean glass jar. Cover the surface with a little oil to seal it, and screw the lid on tightly. It will keep in the fridge for up to 3 months.

Garlic Dipping Sauce V *Thailand*

Preparation time: 15–20 minutes

SERVES 4

1 cup sugar
2/3 cup water
2/3 cup white vinegar
3 cloves garlic, crushed
1 teaspoon sea salt
1 teaspoon chili powder
1 tablespoon freshly chopped coriander

Mix the sugar, water, vinegar, garlic, and salt in a medium saucepan. Bring the mixture to a boil, stirring to dissolve the sugar. Then reduce the heat and simmer until the sauce thickens slightly, for about 10–15 minutes.

Remove the pan from the heat, and add the chili powder and coriander. Allow the mixture to cool a little before serving.

Skorthalia (Thick Garlic Sauce) V *Greece*

Preparation time: 10–15 minutes

SERVES 4

1/3 cup crustless white bread, soaked in water and squeezed out
3 cloves garlic, crushed
1 tablespoon white wine vinegar
pinch of sea salt
6 tablespoons olive oil
3 tablespoons ground almonds or walnuts
2 tablespoons cold water (optional)

Place the damp bread in a blender. Add the garlic, vinegar, and a pinch of salt, and blend until smooth. While the blender is still running, add the olive oil in a thin stream. Then add the nuts and blend again. Add the water or a little more oil if necessary to thin out the sauce—it should be the consistency of Greek yogurt.

Yogurt with Fresh Mint V *Lebanon*

Preparation time: 35 minutes (plus 30 minutes)

SERVES 4–6

4 tablespoons fresh, finely chopped mint
1 1/4 cups plain dairy or soy yogurt
lemon juice to taste
sea salt and black pepper to taste

Mix the chopped mint into the yogurt and season to taste with a little lemon juice, salt, and pepper. Allow the sauce to sit for at least half an hour, so that the flavor of the mint permeates the yogurt.

Tahini Citrus Sauce V *Greece*

Preparation time: 5 minutes (plus 30 minutes)

SERVES 4–6

6 tablespoons tahini (sesame paste)
3 tablespoons fresh orange juice
6 tablespoons fresh lemon juice

Combine the ingredients and allow the sauce to sit for at least half an hour.

Cranberry Sauce V *USA*

SERVES 8

Preparation time: 10 minutes

1 pound fresh or frozen cranberries
1 large thin-skinned orange (Seville if available)
1 cup superfine sugar

Wash the cranberries and check them for stems. Put them in a blender. Slice both ends off the orange, but leave the rest of the peel on. Cut the orange into small pieces and remove the seeds. Place the orange pieces in the blender with the cranberries. Add the sugar and purée to an even consistency. Chill in the fridge before serving.

Satay Sauce V *Thailand*

SERVES 4

Preparation time: 5 minutes

¾ cup chunky peanut butter
1–2 cloves garlic, crushed
1 teaspoon chili powder
¾ cup vegetable stock (page 32), warmed

Mix the first three ingredients together in a small bowl and slowly stir in the stock.

Arugula and Herb Pesto ~ *Italy*

SERVES 2–4

Preparation time: 10 minutes

4 tablespoons freshly chopped arugula
4 tablespoons freshly chopped coriander
2 tablespoons freshly chopped flat leaf parsley
1 teaspoon chopped red chili pepper
4 tablespoons olive oil
1 tablespoon sesame oil
1 tablespoon vegetable stock (page 32)
1 tablespoon pine nuts, chopped finely
¾ cup vegetarian pecorino cheese, grated
sea salt and black pepper to taste

Combine the ingredients in a medium bowl until well mixed. Serve with pasta or gnocchi (potato dumplings).

Pesto Sauce ~ *Italy*

SERVES 2

Preparation time: 5 minutes

6 tablespoons freshly chopped basil
2 large cloves garlic, crushed
⅔ cup pine nuts or walnuts, chopped
½ cup vegetarian Parmesan, grated
⅔ cup olive oil
sea salt and black pepper to taste

In a medium bowl, mix the basil, garlic, nuts, and cheese. Stir in the olive oil and season to taste with salt and pepper.

Green Curry Paste V *Thailand*

Preparation time:
25 minutes

MAKES 8 TABLESPOONS

2 long chili peppers, seeded and chopped
6 small green chili peppers, seeded and chopped
1 stalk lemon grass, chopped
3 small shallots, chopped
4 cloves garlic, chopped
1-inch galingale, or fresh ginger, chopped
4 teaspoons freshly chopped coriander
1 teaspoon ground coriander
½ teaspoon ground cumin
½ teaspoon ground white or black pepper
grated zest of 2 small limes, or 1 teaspoon chopped kaffir lime leaves
2 teaspoons sea salt

In a small blender (or using a mortar and pestle), blend all of the ingredients together to make a smooth paste.

Roasted Red Pepper Sauce V *Spain*

Cooking time:
45 minutes

SERVES 6

5 red bell peppers
2 large tomatoes
1–2 tablespoons olive oil
2–3 tablespoons crème fraîche or warmed soy cream
sea salt and black pepper to taste

Put the peppers and tomatoes on a baking sheet and roast them at 400°F for 20–30 minutes, turning them from time to time until the peppers have blackened and the tomatoes have cooked. Cool the peppers in a paper bag for 10 minutes, then peel off the skins, core, and seed them. Skin the tomatoes.

Put the peppers and tomatoes in a blender with the olive oil. Blend to a purée. Pour into a small saucepan, add the crème fraîche or soy cream, and season to taste with salt and pepper. Stir well and heat before serving.

Special Gravy V *UK*

Preparation time:
25 minutes

SERVES 3–4

2 tablespoons olive oil
1 medium onion, chopped finely
1½ cups mushrooms, chopped small
2 teaspoons tomato purée
2 tablespoons vegetarian gravy mix
2 cups vegetable stock (page 32), or water
sea salt and black pepper to taste

In a medium saucepan, heat the oil and cook the onion until it is golden brown, for 5–6 minutes. Stir in the mushrooms and cook until soft, a further 5 minutes, stirring. Add the tomato purée.

Sprinkle the gravy mix into the pan, stir well, then add the stock or water slowly, stirring all the time. Bring to a boil, then simmer gently for 5 minutes. Season to taste with salt and pepper before serving.

Tomato Coulis ⓥ *UK*

MAKES 2 1/2 CUPS

Preparation time: ***15–20 minutes***

1 pound ripe plum tomatoes, skinned and chopped (page 121)
1 large onion, chopped
4 medium stalks celery, chopped
paprika to taste
1 tablespoon soy sauce (optional)
2 teaspoons sugar
1 tablespoon freshly chopped rosemary

Put the tomatoes, onion, and celery in a large saucepan and simmer, uncovered, for 5 minutes, stirring continuously. Add the rest of the ingredients and simmer, covered, for a further 10–15 minutes, stirring occasionally, until the vegetables have softened. Blend in a food processor or force through a sieve to make a smooth sauce.

Curry Sauce ⓥ *India*

SERVES 3–4

Preparation time: ***15 minutes***

1 small onion, chopped
2 teaspoons vegetable oil
1 teaspoon curry powder
1 teaspoon tomato purée
2/3 cup vegetable stock (page 32)
2/3 cup dairy or warmed soy milk
1 teaspoon cornstarch
juice of 1/2 lemon
2–3 teaspoons mango or apple chutney

In a medium saucepan, fry the chopped onion in the oil until soft. Add the curry powder and tomato purée, and stir gently. Add the vegetable stock, milk, and cornstarch, and bring to a boil, stirring continuously until the sauce thickens. Add the lemon juice and chutney, and simmer for a further 5 minutes. Strain through a sieve or blend in a food processor before serving.

Salsa Verde ⓥ *Mexico*

SERVES 6

Preparation time: ***15 minutes***

2–3 jalapeño peppers, stems and seeds removed, fresh or preserved
3/4 pound tomatilloes or green (unripe) tomatoes, skinned and chopped (page 121)
1 medium onion, chopped small
1 teaspoon sugar
4 tablespoons freshly chopped coriander (or flat leaf parsley if preferred)
juice of 1 lime
sea salt and black pepper to taste

Finely chop the jalapeños, discarding the seeds if they are fresh.

In a medium saucepan, cook the tomatilloes or tomatoes, onion, and jalapeños in 1/2 inch of water over medium heat for about 5 minutes until they have softened. Let them cool, stir in the remaining ingredients, and season to taste with salt and pepper.

Salsa V *Mexico*

Preparation time:
5–10 minutes

SERVES 4

14-ounce can chopped tomatoes, or 1 pound fresh, skinned and diced (page 121)
1 small or ½ medium red onion, chopped
2 mild green chili peppers, chopped finely
2 teaspoons lemon juice
pinch of sugar if required
2 tablespoons freshly chopped coriander (or flat leaf parsley if preferred)

Mix all the ingredients together and season to taste.

Onion and Juniper Gravy V *UK*

Preparation time:
40–45 minutes

SERVES 4–6

2 small onions, chopped
2 tablespoons (¼ stick) butter or margarine
½ cup red wine
3 tablespoons vegetarian gravy mix
12 juniper berries, crushed finely
2½ cups vegetable stock (page 32)
sea salt and black pepper to taste

In a medium saucepan, sauté the onions in the butter or margarine until golden. Add the wine and bring to a boil.

Add the gravy mix and juniper berries, and slowly stir in the stock. Simmer uncovered for 10 minutes, stirring occasionally. Season to taste with salt and pepper.

Classic Vinaigrette V *France*

Preparation time:
5 minutes
(plus 30 minutes)

SERVES 4

1–2 teaspoons fine or grainy mustard
2 tablespoons fresh lemon or lime juice, or 2 tablespoons wine, balsamic, or cider vinegar
6 tablespoons olive oil
crushed garlic to taste (optional)
sea salt and black pepper to taste

In a small bowl, mix the mustard with the lemon or lime juice or vinegar. Whisk in the olive oil gradually. Stir in the garlic if you are using it. Season to taste with salt and pepper.

Creole Vinaigrette V *USA*

Preparation time:
5 minutes

MAKES 1 CUP

¼ cup red wine vinegar
1 tablespoon mustard
1 clove garlic, crushed
1-2 teaspoons Cajun Spice Mix (page 152)
½ teaspoon cayenne pepper
Tabasco to taste
sea salt and black pepper to taste
¾ cup olive oil

Combine all the ingredients except the oil in a small bowl. Gradually whisk in the oil until the mixture thickens. It will keep in a covered jar in the fridge for up to ten days.

Spicy Pecan Mix ♥ *USA*

MAKES APPROXIMATELY 1 POUND

Preparation time:
10 minutes

1 pound shelled pecan pieces
2 tablespoons vegetable oil
1 tablespoon Cajun Spice Mix (below)
1–2 teaspoons sea salt
⅓ cup each sunflower seeds and pumpkin seeds
2 tablespoons tamari or soy sauce

Mix all the ingredients together in a roasting pan and roast at 350°F for 20 minutes. Allow the nuts to cool. This mix will keep in an airtight container for several weeks. Use it as a salad topping or serve it with drinks.

Cajun Spice Mix ♥ *USA*

MAKES APPROXIMATELY 4 TABLESPOONS

Preparation time:
5 minutes

1 tablespoon paprika
1½ teaspoons black pepper
2–3 teaspoons cayenne pepper or to taste
1 tablespoon garlic powder

Mix the spices together in a small bowl, and store the mix in an airtight container.

Dumplings ♥ *Germany*

MAKES 8

Preparation time:
25–30 minutes

1 cup all-purpose flour
2 teaspoons baking powder
4 tablespoons vegetarian shortening
1 tablespoon dried mixed herbs, or freshly chopped basil
sea salt and black pepper to taste
water to bind

Sift the flour and baking powder, mix it with the shortening, herbs, and salt and pepper, add enough cold water to form a soft manageable dough. Shape the dough into eight dumplings and cook them in simmering stock or soup for 20–25 minutes.

Croûtons ♥ *France*

MAKES 1 CUP

Preparation time:
20–25 minutes

3 medium slices day-old bread
4–5 tablespoons olive oil
garlic powder to taste

Cut the crusts off the bread and cut the slices into small dice. Place them in a medium bowl, drizzle with the oil, sprinkle with garlic powder, and toss well.

Roast the croûtons at 400°F for 15–20 minutes, turning occasionally, until they are golden and crisp.

Chestnut Stuffing V *UK*

Preparation time: ***10 minutes***

Cooking time: ***20–25 minutes***

SERVES 6–8

1¾ cups canned chestnut purée
3 stalks celery, chopped finely
1 medium onion, chopped finely
1½ cups brown breadcrumbs
1 tablespoon freshly chopped sage
1 tablespoon dried mixed herbs
soy sauce to taste

In a medium bowl, mix all the ingredients together thoroughly. Shape the stuffing into walnut-size balls and place them evenly on a greased baking sheet. Bake at 375°F for 20–25 minutes until the balls are crisp.

Herby Stuffing V *USA*

Preparation time: ***15 minutes***

Cooking time: ***30–40 minutes***

SERVES 4–6

1 medium onion, chopped finely
6 small stalks celery, chopped
1 tablespoon each freshly chopped parsley, sage, and thyme
6 tablespoons olive oil
small loaf wholegrain bread, diced
3 tablespoons each roughly chopped pecans, cashews, and brazil nuts
soy sauce or tamari to taste
a little stock or water to bind

In a medium bowl, combine all the ingredients.

Mix well, adding a little stock or water to moisten the mixture. Press the mixture into a greased loaf pan. Bake at 350°F for 30–40 minutes. Allow the stuffing to cool a little before turning it out. Serve it cut into slices.

Easy Shortcrust Pastry V

Preparation time: ***15 minutes (plus chilling time)***

MAKES ½ POUND

1½ cups all-purpose flour
large pinch of fine sea salt
6 tablespoons butter or margarine
3 tablespoons ice water

Sift the flour and salt into a medium bowl and rub in the butter or margarine, lifting the mixture to incorporate as much air as possible. When the mixture resembles fine breadcrumbs, bind it with water. Knead lightly on a floured surface until smooth. Wrap and chill for a minimum of 30 minutes before rolling it out.

Sweetcrust Pastry V

Preparation time: 20 minutes (plus chilling time)

MAKES 3/4 POUND

2 cups all-purpose flour
1 tablespoon superfine sugar
8 tablespoons (1 stick) butter or margarine
1/2 teaspoon natural vanilla extract
3 tablespoons ice cold water

Sift the flour into a large bowl and stir in the sugar. Rub in the butter or margarine lightly until the mixture resembles fine breadcrumbs. Add the vanilla extract and bind with the water. Knead lightly on a floured surface. Wrap and chill for a minimum of 30 minutes before rolling it out.

Crunchy Wholemeal Pastry V

Don't be put off by the unusual ingredients! This is a deliciously light and crunchy pastry that is worth a try even if you are not a vegan.

Preparation time 20 minutes (plus chilling time)

MAKES 3/4 POUND

2 cups wholemeal flour (organic if possible)
8 tablespoons (1 stick) margarine
2 tablespoons sesame seeds
1 tablespoon soy sauce
2 tablespoons ice cold water

Place the flour in a large bowl. Rub the margarine into the flour until it resembles fine breadcrumbs. Stir in the sesame seeds and then bind the dry mixture with soy sauce and cold water. Knead lightly on a floured surface, then wrap and chill for a minimum of 30 minutes before rolling it out.

Desserts, Cakes, and Cookies

Spiced Fruit Filo Parcels V *Greece*

These deliciously moist and sticky little pastries were inspired by the traditional Greek baklava. Serve them with Greek yogurt.

Preparation time: ***25 minutes (plus soaking time)***

Cooking time: ***40 minutes***

MAKES APPROXIMATELY 15

¼ pound sultanas (golden raisins)
3–4 tablespoons Amaretto liqueur or orange juice
2 cups macadamias, pistachios, or almonds, toasted (page 70) and chopped
1 teaspoon ground cinnamon
2 teaspoons ground allspice
1 tablespoon vanilla extract
⅓ pound sheets filo pastry cut into 6-inch squares
¼ cup margarine, melted
1 pound sugar
1¼ cups water
juice and pared zest of 1 lemon
1 cinnamon stick

Place the sultanas in a medium bowl, pour the Amaretto or orange juice over them and leave them to soak for a couple of hours.

Mix in the chopped nuts, spices, and vanilla extract.

Brush a sheet of filo with melted margarine. Spoon a heaped tablespoon of the nut mixture into the center, fold in the edges, and roll it up. Brush the top with more margarine and place on a greased baking sheet. Repeat this process until you have used up all the nut mixture.

Bake at 350°F for 40 minutes until golden brown.

Meanwhile, make the syrup by dissolving the sugar in the water over low heat, then boil it with the lemon juice and zest and the cinnamon stick for 5–6 minutes, until it is thin and sticky. When the pastries have cooked, pour the syrup over them through a sieve. Let them cool completely, turning occasionally so that they are evenly soaked in the syrup. Serve cold.

TIP
A lemon zester is a wonderfully useful piece of equipment. Small and simple, cheap and easily available, it scrapes the zest finely and easily and works far better than a grater, which tends to dig into the pith.

Fruit Flan V *Belgium*

Preparation time: ***45 minutes***

SERVES 6–8

9-inch pie dish, lined with Sweetcrust Pastry (page 154)
¼ cup unsweetened chocolate, melted
2½ cups Crème Pâtissière (page 163)
¼ pound green or black seedless grapes, washed
2 bananas, peeled and sliced
¼ pound each raspberries and redcurrants, washed
3–4 tablespoons apricot jam, warmed and sieved

Bake the pie shell blind (page 161) and let it cool. Brush the base and sides with chocolate and chill until it has set.

Spread the crème pâtissière over the bottom of the pie shell. Arrange the prepared fruit decoratively in concentric circles on top.

Brush the warmed apricot jam glaze on top of the fruit. Allow it to cool completely before serving.

Sopapillas (Sweet Tortilla Fritters) V *Mexico*

Preparation time:
15 minutes

These little Mexican doughnuts can be served drizzled with maple syrup or honey and dusted with sugar and cinnamon.

SERVES 4 (MAKES 8 LARGE SOPAPILLAS)

2 cups all-purpose flour
1 teaspoon salt
2 teaspoons baking powder
2 tablespoons (½ stick) margarine
¾ cup cold water
vegetable oil for deep frying
superfine or confectioners' sugar and honey or maple syrup to serve

Sift the flour, salt, and baking powder into a large bowl. Rub in the margarine until crumbly. Work in the water to form a pastry-like dough.

Knead lightly on a floured surface until smooth, then roll it into a circle ⅛ inch thick. Cut it into 8 triangles.

Pour 2–3 inches of oil into a medium saucepan and place over medium to high heat. The oil is ready when a cube of bread browns immediately. Deep-fry the dough triangles a few at a time until they puff up and become a light golden color, turning them so that they cook evenly, for about 3–4 minutes. Remove them carefully from the oil and drain on paper towels.

Serve dusted with sugar or drizzled with honey or maple syrup.

Apple Pancakes V *The Netherlands*

Preparation time:
30–40 minutes

Dutch pancakes are legendary for their size and golden crispness, with whole restaurants devoted to savory and sweet *pannekoeken*. For these smaller fruit pancakes, use a tart apple such as Granny Smith.

SERVES 4–6

3 large apples, peeled, cored, and coarsely grated
⅔ cup lemon juice
1½ cups all-purpose flour
2 teaspoons baking powder
pinch of sea salt
¾ cup dairy or soy milk
¾ cup water
2 tablespoons vegetable oil
2 teaspoons sugar
vegetable oil for shallow frying
superfine sugar and ground cinnamon to serve

Marinate the apples in the lemon juice for 20 minutes, then drain thoroughly.

Sift the flour, baking powder, and salt into a large bowl. Stir in the milk to make a smooth batter, then beat in the water, oil, and sugar. Finally, fold in the apples.

Heat ¼ inch of oil in a large frying pan until it is hot. Spoon in 3–4 tablespoons of batter at a time to make each pancake. Fry until it is crisp and golden on both sides, for about 1–2 minutes. Drain on paper towels and serve sprinkled with sugar and cinnamon.

Rhubarb Fool (V) *Ireland*

When selecting your rhubarb, choose young, pink stems rather than older ones, which will be thick, stringy, and acidic.

Preparation time: ***30 minutes***

SERVES 4

1½ pounds rhubarb, cut into small pieces
1 cup light brown sugar
¼ teaspoon ground cloves
2 tablespoons fresh orange juice
½ teaspoon grated orange zest
1½ teaspoons vanilla extract
1¼ cups heavy whipping cream, lightly whipped, or 1 cup silken tofu and 5 tablespoons soy cream, blended together
Grand Marnier (optional)

Put the rhubarb, sugar, cloves, and orange juice with the zest in a medium saucepan and cook it gently for 10–15 minutes, stirring occasionally.

Remove the pan from the heat and add the vanilla extract. Let it cool, then chill it in the fridge until it is completely cold.

Combine the tofu mixture or whipped cream with Grand Marnier to taste. Fold this into the cold rhubarb so that it has a marbled effect, or ripple it. Spoon the fool into individual glasses and chill it in the fridge.

TIP
Never eat raw rhubarb or the leaves, which are poisonous. It keeps i the fridge for only a day or two before it becomes limp.

Ice Cream Cake (V) *USA*

Use any combination of your favorite ice cream or sorbet.

Preparation time: ***25 minutes (plus freezing time***

SERVES 8

1 Lemon Sponge Cake (page 180)
3 flavors (and colors) of soy ice cream or sorbet, about ¾ cup of each
2 x Icing (page 180)

Line a 7-inch deep cake pan with wax paper so that it overhangs the edges. Cut the cake into ½-inch slices and press them into the base and around the sides of the pan.

Fill the center with ice cream and/or sorbet scoops. Press them down hard to fit in as much as possible. Place the cake pan in the freezer for a minimum of 1 hour.

When the cake is firm, turn it upside down onto a plate, remove the cake pan, and peel off the wax paper. Spread the top and sides with icing and freeze for a further 20 minutes. Serve immediately.

Rhubarb Fool

Coconut Rice Pudding ⓥ *Thailand*

Preparation time:
40 minutes

The coconut milk gives this unusual rice pudding an exotic flavor. It is particularly good served with a swirl of mango coulis made by puréeing two ripe mangoes with 2 tablespoons of confectioners' sugar.

SERVES 5–6

½ cup long-grain or jasmine rice
1¾ cups canned coconut milk
3 cups dairy or soy milk, plus 2 tablespoons
½ cup sugar
pinch of sea salt
1 teaspoon vanilla extract
1 cup dried coconut
shredded coconut to decorate

Mix the rice, coconut milk, milk, sugar, and a pinch of salt in a large saucepan. Bring to a boil, and stir continuously, then simmer gently for about 25 minutes, stirring frequently.

Stir in the vanilla and dried coconut, and simmer for a further 5 minutes.

Serve warm or cold with a swirl of mango coulis and sprinkled with shredded coconut that has been toasted in a dry frying pan over gentle heat.

Honey Pudding ⓥ *Greece*

Preparation time:
25 minutes

This is a good way of using up leftover bread. As an alternative to honey, you can serve it with maple syrup for vegans.

SERVES 4

12 slices stale bread, cut into circles
1¼ cups dairy or soy milk, plus 5 tablespoons
3 tablespoons vegetable oil
3 tablespoons cornstarch
½ teaspoon baking powder
pinch of sea salt
6 tablespoons (¾ stick) margarine
¾ cup shelled pistachios, chopped
warmed honey or maple syrup to serve

Soak the circles of bread in 1¼ cups milk for a few seconds until they are soft but not mushy, then set them aside.

In a medium bowl, combine the oil, cornstarch, baking powder, remaining 5 tablespoons of milk, and a pinch of salt, and beat well. Melt the margarine in a large frying pan over medium heat. Dip the circles of bread into the batter and fry them until they are crisp and golden on each side, for about 1–2 minutes.

Serve warm, sprinkled with chopped pistachios, and with honey or maple syrup poured on top.

Grandma's Apple Pie V *USA*

Preparation time:
25 minutes

Cooking time:
35–40 minutes

This home-baked apple pie is delicious served at Thanksgiving as an alternative to pumpkin pie.

SERVES 8

3/4 cup butter or margarine, softened
3/4 cup low-fat cream cheese
3 cups all-purpose flour
2 pounds apples, peeled, cored, and sliced thinly
2 tablespoons ground cinnamon
5–6 tablespoons sugar, to taste, depending on the sweetness of the apples
2 tablespoons lemon juice

In a medium bowl, beat the butter or margarine and cream cheese together until smooth. Work in the flour to make a soft dough. Divide the dough into two balls, wrap them, and chill them in the fridge for a minimum of 1 hour.

Mix the sliced apples with the cinnamon, sugar, and lemon juice, reserving a little sugar and cinnamon. Mix well.

On a lightly floured surface, roll out one ball of pastry and use it to line a deep 10-inch pie dish. Bake the pastry blind (see below).

When the pie shell has cooled, fill it with the apples, piling them higher in the center.

Roll out the other pastry ball thinly and gently lay it on top. Press the edges together, trim off any excess pastry, then mark the edges with a fork and prick the top of the pie several times.

Mix the reserved cinnamon and sugar together, and sprinkle the mixture on top of the pie. Bake at 375°F for 35–40 minutes, until the topping is golden brown and the apples have cooked.

TIP
If the pie begins to brown too early, cover it loosely with foil.

BAKING BLIND

Baking blind, which partially cooks the pie shell, will ensure that it stays crisp under a liquid filling. Cover the pastry, including the rim, with aluminum foil to prevent it from rising. Weigh it down with baking beans (dried lima or butter beans are perfect). Bake it in a preheated oven at 400°F for 10–12 minutes (slightly less time is needed if you are making small individual pie shells). Remove the foil and bake for a further 5 minutes or until the pie shell starts to color.

Pecan Roulade ~ *USA*

Preparation time: ***50 minutes***

Cooking time: ***20–25 minutes***

This is a sophisticated version of a jelly roll that is made with a pecan cake base. It is easier to make than you might think.

SERVES 8

6 large organic eggs, separated
1½ cups superfine sugar, plus 2 tablespoons
2¼ cups pecans, chopped finely
1 teaspoon baking powder
1¼ cups heavy whipping cream
1 teaspoon vanilla extract
½ pound raspberries or strawberries, washed and trimmed
confectioners' sugar to decorate

Grease a 9 x 13-inch jelly roll sheet and line it with wax paper.

In a large bowl, whisk the egg yolks with 1½ cups of sugar until the mixture turns pale yellow. Fold in the pecans and the baking powder.

Whisk the egg whites until they become stiff. Stir 2–3 tablespoons of the whites into the nut mixture, then gently fold in the rest.

Spread the mixture onto the baking sheet, level the surface, and bake at 350°F for 20–25 minutes until it is just firm to the touch. Cover with a lightly dampened tea towel and leave it for 15 minutes, then chill in the fridge for a further 15 minutes.

Whip the cream with the vanilla extract and the extra 2 tablespoons of sugar until it becomes thick. Finally, gently fold in the berries.

Carefully turn the chilled sponge onto the tea towel. Gently peel off the paper.

Spread the whipped cream onto the pecan cake and roll it up using the tea towel. Dust with confectioners' sugar before serving.

Crème Pâtissière V *France*

Preparation time: ***5–10 minutes***

MAKES 2½ CUPS

4 tablespoons cornstarch
8 tablespoons superfine sugar
pinch of sea salt
2¼ cups soy milk
2 tablespoons vegetable oil
1 tablespoon vanilla extract
2 tablespoons Grand Marnier (optional)

In a medium bowl, combine the cornstarch, sugar, and a pinch of salt with enough cold milk to make a paste.

In a medium saucepan, heat the remaining milk to boiling point, and gradually pour it into the paste, stirring continuously. Return it to the saucepan and heat it gently over low heat, stirring, until it thickens. Let it bubble very gently for 2–3 minutes to cook the cornstarch.

Finally, stir in the vegetable oil, vanilla extract, and Grand Marnier, and let the crème cool before using it.

ecan Roulade

Mississippi Mud Pie ~ *USA*

It is unclear how this pie got its name, as it isn't originally from Mississippi. Perhaps someone thought the rich layers of chocolate mousse and caramel on a cookie base looked like the mud flats along America's most famous river!

Preparation time: ***60 minutes (plus chilling time)***

SERVES 12

2 tablespoons coffee granules
3/4 cup condensed milk
3/4 cup unsalted butter, melted
3/4 cup graham crackers, crushed
3/4 cup ginger cookies, crushed
1 cup unsweetened chocolate, broken into squares
2 large organic eggs, separated
2/3 cup heavy cream
8 tablespoons (1 stick) butter or margarine
1/2 cup sugar
1 teaspoon light maple syrup
2 medium bananas
chocolate curls to decorate
2 teaspoons cocoa powder

Grease an 8-inch cake pan with a removable base. In a small bowl, mix the coffee granules into the condensed milk, stir well, and put it to one side.

Mix the melted butter with the crushed graham crackers and cookies. Press the mixture into the pan so that it covers the bottom and sides evenly. Put it in the fridge to chill for a minimum of 30 minutes.

Melt the chocolate in a bowl over a pan of hot water. Remove it from the heat and allow it to cool slightly, then beat in the egg yolks and the cream. Whisk the egg whites until they become stiff and fold them into the chocolate mixture. Pour the filling into the prepared cookie base and chill for at least 2 hours.

Place the condensed milk and coffee mixture in a medium saucepan with the butter or margarine, sugar, andsyrup. Melt the ingredients slowly over low heat. When melted, increase the heat to medium, stirring continuously. Bring to a gentle boil and cook for 5 more minutes, stirring continuously. Be careful that the mixture doesn't stick to the base of the pan and burn.

You can test it by dropping a little of the mixture in some cold water on a saucer—if it stays in a soft ball, it is ready. Remove the pan from the heat and allow the sauce to cool, beating it now and then. Spread the sauce over the chocolate mixture in the pan and chill for a minimum of 3 hours.

Remove the pie carefully from the pan. Decorate it with circles of sliced bananas, cover with the chocolate curls, and dust with sifted cocoa powder.

Fruit Soufflés with Coulis ~ *France*

Preparation time: ***15 minutes***

Cooking time: ***12–15 minutes***

These deliciously light soufflés are served with a fruit coulis and/or crème fraîche.

SERVES 6

1 tablespoon butter, melted
confectioners' sugar for dusting
1½ pounds prepared mixed fruit, such as raspberries, strawberries, apricots, peaches, bananas, kiwi, blackberries
1 teaspoon vanilla extract
6 large organic eggs, separated
1–2 tablespoons confectioners' sugar
6–7 tablespoons superfine sugar

Lightly butter six individual soufflé dishes and sprinkle them with a little confectioners' sugar.

Purée the fruit, and mix in the vanilla extract. To make the coulis, take half of this mixture, stir in the confectioners' sugar, and chill.

Whisk the egg whites until stiff. Gradually whisk in the superfine sugar until the mixture becomes thick and glossy.

Beat the egg yolks and mix with the remaining fruit purée. Stir in 2–3 tablespoons of the egg whites, then fold in the rest gently. Pour the mixture into the prepared dishes and bake at 400°F for about 12–15 minutes or until the soufflés have risen and browned lightly. Serve immediately with the coulis and/or crème fraîche.

TIP
It is possible to sieve the purée to get rid of the berry seeds, but I prefer to leave them in.

Key Lime Pie ~ *USA*

Preparation time: ***30 minutes (plus freezing time)***

This wonderfully refreshing dessert is a local specialty in the Florida Keys, where particularly tart limes grow semi-wild.

SERVES 6

¾ cup graham crackers
2 tablespoons superfine sugar
¼ cup melted butter or margarine
3 large organic egg yolks, beaten
14-ounce can condensed milk
juice of 3 large limes
finely grated zest of 1 large lime
⅔ cup heavy cream, whipped
slices of lime to decorate

Crush the crackers to fine crumbs in a large bowl. Stir in the sugar, then mix thoroughly with the melted butter or margarine. Press the mixture into a greased 8-inch cake pan and chill for at least 30 minutes in the fridge.

In a medium bowl, beat the egg yolks until creamy. Slowly beat in the condensed milk and stir in the lime juice and zest. Pour the mixture into the cake pan and freeze it until firm, for 2–3 hours.

When you are ready to serve, remove the pie from the freezer and decorate it with whipped cream and lime slices. It does not freeze hard and is delectable eaten this cold.

Panna Cotta with Raspberry Coulis ~ *Italy*

SERVES 6

Preparation time:
1 hour 15 minutes
(plus chilling time)

1 pound raspberries
1 cup confectioners' sugar
5 cups heavy cream
2 vanilla beans, split
pared zest of 2 lemons
1/4 cup brandy (optional)

Purée the berries in a blender with 2 tablespoons of the sugar, then strain the purée through a sieve to remove the seeds. Divide the coulis among six dessert bowls.

Pour 3 cups of the cream into a wide, shallow pan, add the vanilla beans and lemon zest, and bring to a boil slowly over low heat. Simmer until the mixture has reduced by half, for about 45 minutes.

Remove the lemon zest and allow the mixture to cool. Then remove the vanilla beans and squeeze the seeds into the cream.

Whip the remaining cream with the remaining sugar until thick and fold it into the cooled vanilla cream. Stir in the brandy to taste and pour the cream over the coulis in the bowls. Chill for at least 2 hours before serving. Decorate with extra fruit.

Coconut Pie ~ *Caribbean*

When we were recording the *Tug of War* album, we spent a lot of time in the Caribbean and this unusual pudding soon became one of my favorites.

Preparation time:
15 minutes

Cooking time:
15–20 minutes

SERVES 4–6

9-inch cake pan lined with Sweetcrust Pastry (page 154)
3 tablespoons cornstarch
6 tablespoons superfine sugar
1 3/4 cups dairy or soy milk
1 tablespoon butter or margarine
1 teaspoon vanilla extract
2 teaspoons ground allspice
1 cup dried coconut
2 large organic eggs, separated

Bake the pie shell blind (page 161) and leave it to cool. Meanwhile, mix the cornstarch with 4 tablespoons of the sugar and enough cold milk to make a paste. Warm the remaining milk with the butter or margarine in a small pan. Gradually stir the warm milk into the paste. Return the mixture to the pan and cook gently until it thickens, stirring continuously.

Add the vanilla, allspice, and coconut, and stir for 2 minutes. Remove from the heat and allow it to cool slightly before beating in the egg yolks.

Whisk the egg whites until stiff, then whisk in the remaining sugar until they become thick and glossy. Stir 2 tablespoons of the egg whites into the coconut mixture, then fold in the rest. Pour the filling into the pie shell and bake at 350°F for 15–20 minutes until the pie has browned lightly and set in the center.

Panna Cotta
with Raspberry Coulis

Naughty Nougat Cake ~ *Norway*

Preparation time:
30 minutes

Cooking time:
45 minutes

This is a cake that my friend, Helge, made for me. He usually makes it for special occasions like birthdays, weddings, and Christmas, but it is amazing how many other excuses to make it we can find!

SERVES 10–12

1¼ cups ground almonds
2½ cups confectioners' sugar
6 large organic egg whites
4 tablespoons (½ stick) butter or margarine
¼ cup unsweetened chocolate, broken into pieces
2 tablespoons strong black coffee
2 large organic egg yolks
2 tablespoons shredded almonds, toasted (page 70) to decorate

Sift the almonds and 2 cups of the confectioners' sugar into a large bowl.

Whisk the egg whites until stiff. Stir a quarter of them into the almond and sugar mixture, then gently fold in the rest.

Put the mixture into a well-greased 9-inch round cake pan and bake at 350°F for about 45 minutes. Allow the cake to cool, then turn it out onto a plate.

Meanwhile, make the icing by creaming the butter or margarine with the remaining sugar until it turns a thick and creamy pale yellow.

Melt the chocolate with the coffee in a bowl over a pan of hot water. Remove the bowl from the heat and put it in the fridge for 10 minutes. Next, beat the egg yolks into the butter and sugar until it turns pale and creamy, then add the chilled chocolate and coffee mixture and beat until smooth.

When the cake is completely cool, decorate it with the icing. If you are confident enough to use an icing bag do so, but if not, simply spread the topping over the top and sides of the cakes using a wet knife and finish it off with a sprinkling of almonds.

Exotic Fruit Platter V *India*

This dish takes advantage of the many types of interesting and exotic fruit now available. It is so simple to assemble, but with a bit of imagination and creativity it makes an exquisite finale to any dinner party. Served with a delicious vegan crème anglaise, it is a winner for vegans and non-vegans alike.

Preparation time: ***30 minutes***

SERVES 6–8

4½ pounds fruit, such as pineapple, passion fruit, watermelon, starfruit
½ cup superfine sugar
1¼ cups water
juice of ½ lime
2 teaspoons vanilla extract

Arrange chunks or slices of fruit decoratively on a large serving plate.

In a small saucepan, dissolve the sugar in the water over medium heat, stirring, then turn it into a light syrup by boiling it for 3–4 minutes. Stir in the lime juice and vanilla extract.

Allow the syrup to cool before pouring it over the fruit. Chill for at least 10 minutes before serving it with a jug of crème anglaise.

Crème Anglaise V *France*

MAKES APPROXIMATELY 2 CUPS

Preparation time: ***15 minutes***

2 cups soy milk, plus 2 tablespoons
1 vanilla bean, split
½ cup superfine sugar
3 tablespoons cornstarch
2 tablespoons vegetable oil

In a medium saucepan, warm 2 cups of soy milk with the vanilla bean. Do not allow it to boil. In a medium bowl, mix the sugar, cornstarch, vegetable oil, and remaining milk to a paste. Pour the warm milk into the paste, stirring continuously.

Return this mixture to the saucepan and cook gently over medium heat, stirring continuously. When the sauce begins to thicken and turn creamy, reduce the heat. Don't allow the mixture to boil: it should just bubble gently for 5 more minutes. Remove the vanilla bean and squeeze the seeds into the crème anglaise.

Pour the crème into a jug and serve it warm or cold.

Exotic Fruit Platter with Crème Anglaise

Celebration Pudding ~ *UK*

This is a traditional English steamed fruit pudding with an exotic slant. Serve with cream or with Crème Anglaise (page 170).

Preparation time:
25 minutes
(plus soaking time)

Cooking time:
2 hours

SERVES 6

½ cup dried mango slices
½ cup dried figs
½ cup shredded vegetarian shortening
1 cup all-purpose flour
1 cup breadcrumbs
½ cup light soft brown sugar
2 teaspoons ground cinnamon
2 teaspoons ground ginger
½ cup candied pineapple wedges
¼ cup candied cherries, quartered
2 large organic eggs, beaten
6 tablespoons dairy or soy milk
1 large banana, mashed
3 tablespoons brandy, plus extra for serving
grated zest and juice of 1 lime
1 tablespoon molasses

Cover the mango slices and figs with boiling water and soak them for an hour. Drain, chop, and set them aside.

Grease a 4-cup pudding bowl and place a small circle of wax paper in the bottom.

Put all the dry ingredients in a large bowl. Stir in all the fruit, except the banana, then beat in the eggs, milk, banana, brandy, lime zest and juice, and the molasses. Mix well.

Spoon the mixture into the pudding bowl, cover it with wax paper and aluminum foil, and secure tightly with string.

Place the pudding bowl in a saucepan and fill it up to halfway with boiling water. Steam it for 2 hours, replenishing the pan with hot water as necessary.

Turn the pudding out of the bowl. Just before serving, pour brandy over the top, light it with a match, and bring it flaming to the table. This should be done with great care.

Tarte Tatin ♥ *France*

Preparation time:
25 minutes
(plus chilling time)

Cooking time:
30–35 minutes

This apple flan was created by the Tatin sisters at the Hôtel Terminus Tatin in Lamotte-Beuvron, a small village near Paris. It is traditionally baked with the pastry on top of the fruit and turned upside down before serving.

SERVES 6

PASTRY

2 cups all-purpose flour
2 tablespoons superfine sugar
1/4 teaspoon sea salt
1/4 teaspoon baking powder
1/4 teaspoon ground allspice
6 tablespoons (3/4 stick) butter or margarine
3–4 tablespoons water

FILLING

1 1/2 cups superfine sugar
2/3 cup water
2 pounds dessert apples, cored and sliced
6 tablespoons (3/4 stick) butter or margarine
1 tablespoon lemon juice
1/2 teaspoon grated lemon zest
2 tablespoons malt extract

To make the pastry, sieve the flour, sugar, salt, baking powder, and allspice into a large bowl. Rub in the margarine, then stir in enough water to make a firm dough. Gather it carefully into a ball, wrap, and chill it in the fridge for 1 hour.

To make the filling, gently heat 1 cup of the sugar with the water until the sugar dissolves, then boil it until it turns a rich caramel color. Carefully pour the caramel into a greased 10-inch pie pan.

Gently cook and turn the apple slices in the margarine for 2–3 minutes, then add the lemon juice, zest, 1/2 cup of sugar, and the malt extract, and stir until it has dissolved.

Arrange the apples on top of the caramel in the pie pan. Roll the pastry out on a floured surface until it is big enough to cover the pie pan, allowing an extra 1/2 inch all around. Lay it on top of the apples and press down with a fork.

Bake at 375°F for 30–35 minutes until the pastry is golden and crisp. Let it sit for 5–10 minutes before turning it upside down onto a plate. This is best done quickly and confidently over the sink. Serve warm or cold with cream.

Pear Flan v *France*

There are thousands of varieties of pear—choose your favorite for this lovely flan.

Preparation time: **45 minutes, (plus chilling time)**

Cooking time: **25–30 minutes**

SERVES 6–8

PASTRY

3½ cups all-purpose flour
½ teaspoon sea salt
½ cup confectioners' sugar
½ teaspoon grated lemon zest
¾ cup butter or margarine
½ cup water combined with 1 teaspoon vanilla extract

BASE

⅔ cup pecans, finely chopped
1 cup fresh breadcrumbs
¼ cup light brown sugar
½ teaspoon ground cinnamon

FILLING

2 pounds pears, cored and sliced thinly
3 tablespoons superfine sugar
4 tablespoons (½ stick) margarine, diced
4 tablespoons apricot jam, warmed and sieved
2 tablespoons slivered almonds, toasted (page 70)

To make the pastry, sift the flour and salt into a large bowl and stir in the sugar and lemon zest. Rub in the butter or margarine lightly until the mixture resembles fine breadcrumbs. Bind the ingredients with the water. Knead lightly on a floured surface until smooth. Wrap and chill in the fridge for a minimum of 30 minutes before rolling it out.

Roll out the pastry thinly to fit a 12-inch pie pan. Bake blind (page 161). Allow it to cool.

Combine the ingredients for the base in a medium bowl and sprinkle them over the bottom of the pie shell before adding the pears.

Place the pears in concentric circles, overlapping them so that they spiral into the center. Sprinkle the pears with sugar and dot with the margarine. Bake at 375°F for 25–30 minutes until the pears turn golden.

Glaze the surface of the flan with the warm apricot jam and scatter the slivered almonds on top. Serve it warm or cold.

TIP

Squeeze lemon juice over the pear slices as you finish cutting them so they don't discolor.

ear Flan

Warm Chocolate Soufflés with Bittersweet Sauce ~ *France*

Preparation time: ***20 minutes***

Cooking time: ***20–25 minutes***

Chocolate has been popular in France since the seventeenth century. Like wine, cocoa beans vary in quality and according to the fertility of the cultivation area. They are graded and tested by experts, many of whom are based in Bordeaux. These soufflés are a chocoholic's dream!

SERVES 6

1 cup superfine sugar, plus 6 teaspoons
4 tablespoons unsalted butter
3/4 cup unsweetened chocolate, broken into pieces
pinch of sea salt
4 tablespoons cocoa powder
1 teaspoon vanilla extract
4 medium organic egg whites
confectioners' sugar to decorate
Bittersweet Sauce (see below)

Lightly butter six individual soufflé dishes and sprinkle a teaspoon of sugar into each one. Melt the butter in a medium saucepan and add the chocolate, a pinch of salt, the cocoa powder, and 3 tablespoons of the sugar. Mix until smooth, then remove the pan from the heat and stir in the vanilla extract. Allow it to cool slightly.

Whisk the egg whites until they become stiff, then whisk in the cup of sugar until the mixture becomes thick and glossy. Stir 2–3 tablespoons of the egg whites into the chocolate mixture, then fold in the rest.

Spoon the chocolate mixture into the soufflé dishes, filling each about two-thirds full. Place the dishes on a baking sheet and bake at 400°F for 15–20 minutes, until the soufflés have puffed up and set lightly.

Dust with confectioners' sugar and serve warm or cold.

Bittersweet Sauce V *France*

Preparation time: ***5–10 minutes***

FOR 4–6

1/2 cup strong black coffee
3 tablespoons confectioners' sugar
3/4 cup unsweetened chocolate, broken into pieces
1/2 cup light dairy or warmed soy cream
1 teaspoon vanilla extract

Gently heat the coffee in a heavy-based saucepan over low heat before adding the confectioners' sugar, and continue to heat until it bubbles.

Remove the pan from the heat and add the chocolate. Stir until the chocolate has melted, then stir in the cream and vanilla extract.

Warm Chocolate Soufflés with Bittersweet Sauce

Non-dairy Crème Brulée ~ *France*

A friend of mine is lactose intolerant but adores crème brulée, so I experimented with this version at a dinner party. I hope you agree, as my friend did, that it is a real success.

Preparation time: ***20 minutes*** ***(plus chilling time)***

SERVES 4

4 large organic egg yolks
6–8 tablespoons superfine sugar
2 teaspoons vanilla extract
2½ cups soy cream

In a medium bowl, whisk the egg yolks with 2 tablespoons of sugar until they turn a thick and creamy pale yellow. Add the vanilla extract.

Put the cream into a medium saucepan and heat it over very low heat until just below boiling. Be careful that it doesn't burn.

Gradually pour the cream into the yolk mixture, beating with a whisk. Return the mixture to the pan and heat it gently, stirring with a wooden spoon over very low heat until it just thickens. This will take about 5 minutes. Pour the cream into individual soufflé dishes or ramekins and chill in the fridge until it has set.

Heat the broiler to maximum temperature. Sprinkle the top of each brulée evenly with 1 tablespoon of sugar. Place them under the broiler and allow the sugar to melt and brown a little, before removing. Put them in a cold place to harden the top.

TIP
Soy cream must be handled with loving care when cooking with it—do not be tempted to hurry!

Golden Syrup Pudding V *UK*

Serve this delectable English steamed pudding with as much syrup as your teeth and waistline can handle!

Preparation time: ***20–25 minutes***

Cooking time: ***1½–2 hours***

SERVES 6–8

9 tablespoons light maple syrup, plus extra to serve
1½ cups all-purpose flour
2 cups breadcrumbs
½ cup shredded vegetable shortening
½ cup superfine sugar
2 teaspoons ground ginger
1½ teaspoons baking soda
pinch of sea salt
½ medium banana, mashed
dairy or soy milk

Grease a medium pudding bowl and put 6 tablespoons of syrup in the bottom. In a large bowl, mix the dry ingredients.

In a medium bowl, combine the banana with the rest of the syrup and a little milk. Stir this into the dry mixture, adding more milk as required to bring it to a very soft dropping consistency.

Put the mixture into the pudding bowl, cover the top with wax paper, and secure it with string. Steam the pudding in a large pan of boiling water for 1½–2 hours, topping up the pan with hot water as necessary. Turn the pudding out onto a plate to serve.

Toffee Apples and Bananas ∨ *China*

Preparation time:
30–40 minutes

These caramel-coated fruit pieces make a great finish to any meal, but especially an Oriental one.

SERVES 4

2 tablespoons all-purpose flour
1 tablespoon cornstarch
pinch of sea salt
¼ teaspoon baking powder
¼ cup dairy or soy milk
¼ cup water
1 tablespoon sesame oil
peanut oil for deep frying
2 large, firm apples, peeled, cored, and cut into 8 thick wedges
2 large, firm bananas, peeled and cut into 2-inch chunks
1½ cups superfine sugar
2 tablespoons sesame seeds

Sift the flour, cornstarch, salt, and baking powder into a large bowl, and gradually beat in the soy milk, water, and sesame oil to make a smooth, thick batter.

Pour 2–3 inches of oil into a medium saucepan and place on medium to high heat. The oil is ready when a cube of bread browns immediately. Dip the fruit into the batter in batches and deep-fry for about 2 minutes until golden. Remove with a slotted spoon and drain on paper towels. Repeat until all the fruit is cooked.

Put the sugar, sesame seeds, and 2 tablespoons of the hot oil into a medium saucepan and heat gently until the sugar melts and begins to caramelize. Do not let it get too hot or boil. When it is light brown, add the fruit sections a few at a time to prevent them from sticking and stir them gently in the caramel syrup to coat them. Lift them carefully out onto a plate and allow them to harden for a minute or two before serving.

TIP
Both oil and sugar are volatile when hot, so care should be taken: water must never be added to either until the mixture has cooled.

Lemon Sponge Cake ~~V~~ *UK*

MAKES 2 X 7-INCH ROUNDS

Preparation time: ***25 minutes***

Cooking time: ***25 minutes***

CAKE

2¼ cups all-purpose flour
1½ tablespoons baking powder
½ cup superfine sugar
3 lemons, zest and juice
8 tablespoons (1 stick) margarine
⅓ cup hot water
2 tablespoons malt extract

ICING

4 tablespoons (1 stick) margarine
1 cup confectioners' sugar
1 teaspoon grated lemon zest
2 teaspoons soy cream

FILLING

4 tablespoons apricot jam
walnuts, finely chopped

Grease and line two 7-inch cake pans.

To make the cake, sift the flour, baking powder, and sugar into a large bowl and add the lemon zest. In a small bowl, combine the water, malt extract, and lemon juice. Add this to the flour mixture, beat for a few minutes until smooth, then transfer it to the cake pans. Bake at 400°F for 25 minutes until the cakes are just firm and golden brown.

Meanwhile, make the icing by beating together the margarine, sugar, zest, and cream. Beat well, until it becomes light and fluffy.

Sandwich the two cakes together with apricot jam and half the icing. Spread the remaining icing on top and sprinkle with walnuts.

Pecan Macaroons ~ *USA*

Pecans are absolutely my favorite nuts and I just love them in this recipe as they melt in the mouth.

Preparation time: ***25 minutes***

Cooking time: ***20–25 minutes***

MAKES 20

4 large organic egg whites
2½ cups superfine sugar
2 cups pecans, chopped
2 cups fresh white breadcrumbs
1 teaspoon vanilla extract

In a large bowl, whisk the egg whites until they are stiff, then whisk in the sugar a little at a time until they become glossy. Divide the mixture between two bowls. Stir the nuts and breadcrumbs into one and the vanilla extract into the other.

Spread the nut and crumb mixture on a floured surface and press it flat until it is about ¼ inch thick. Cut out 20 circles with a pastry cutter. Lay the circles on a greased baking sheet and spread each one with some of the reserved vanilla mixture. Bake at 325°F for 20–25 minutes or until they are lightly browned. Leave them to cool on the baking sheet.

Lemon Wafers V *Spain*

Preparation time: **15 minutes**

Cooking time: **8–10 minutes**

Lemon has always been one of my favorite flavors and I use it whenever and wherever I can in my cooking. These light and crisp cookies are just right for serving with ice cream or sorbet.

MAKES ABOUT 28

8 tablespoons (1 stick) butter or margarine, softened
1 cup superfine sugar
1 cup all-purpose flour
½ teaspoon ground ginger
3 tablespoons fresh lemon juice

In a medium bowl, cream the butter or margarine and sugar until it is light and fluffy. Sift the flour and ginger together, add half to the creamed mixture with the lemon juice and beat again. Then add the remaining flour and beat well.

Place teaspoonsfuls of the mixture on a well-greased baking sheet. Leave plenty of room between them, as they spread to about double their size.

Bake at 375°F for 8–10 minutes. The edges should be crisp and the middle pale in color. Remove them from the baking sheet and allow them to cool on a wire rack before lifting them off carefully with a knife.

Butter Crunch Squares V *UK*

Preparation time: **20–25 minutes**

Cooking time: **25–30 minutes**

These squares are almost like granola bars but they have an extra crumbly topping.

MAKES 18

3 cups all-purpose flour
½ pound butter or margarine
1 cup superfine sugar
4 teaspoons ground cinnamon
2 egg yolks and 1 egg white from medium organic eggs
1⅔ cups pecans, coarsely chopped

Sift the flour into a large bowl. Rub in the butter or margarine and stir in ⅔ cup of the sugar. Stir in 3 teaspoons of cinnamon and the egg yolks.

Divide the mixture between two buttered shallow 9-inch square baking pans and press down lightly. Brush the surfaces with lightly beaten egg white. Top with the nuts mixed with the remaining sugar and cinnamon. Bake at 350°F for 20–25 minutes.

Cut the squares while still warm and allow them to cool in the pan. Lift them out carefully before they are cold.

Chocolate Crescents ∨ *Mexico*

These crunchy chocolate cookies taste good in any shape you like—crescents, diamonds, or hearts.

Preparation time: ***20–25 minutes***

Cooking time: ***20 minutes***

MAKES APPROXIMATELY 20 COOKIES

1¼ cups all-purpose flour, sifted
½ cup superfine sugar
pinch of sea salt
6 tablespoons (¾ stick) butter or margarine
¼ cup almonds, blanched, toasted (page 70), and chopped
¼ cup unsweetened chocolate, grated and chilled
1–2 tablespoons dairy or soy milk

In a large bowl, sift the flour with the sugar and a pinch of salt. Rub in the butter or margarine and work it with your fingers until it resembles coarse breadcrumbs.

Add the almonds and the chocolate, and continue to work the mixture until it forms a smooth dough, adding a little milk if necessary.

Roll out the dough thinly on a lightly floured surface and cut it into your desired shape with a cutter. Roll out the trimmings as necessary.

Bake the shapes on a greased cookie sheet at 325°F for 18–20 minutes. Allow them to cool on a wire rack.

Poppy Seed Cookies ∨ *Germany*

These satisfying cookies are particularly good when half-dipped in chocolate.

Preparation time: ***30 minutes***

Cooking time: ***20 minutes***

MAKES 24 COOKIES

⅓ cup dairy or soy milk
¾ cup poppy seeds
4 tablespoons (½ stick) butter or margarine
½ cup superfine sugar
2 tablespoons unsweetened chocolate, melted
½ teaspoon ground cinnamon
¼ teaspoon ground cloves
⅔ cup currants
1¼ cups all-purpose flour
1 teaspoon baking powder

In a small saucepan, heat the milk until it is almost boiling, then remove the pan from the heat and soak the poppy seeds in the milk for about 15 minutes.

In a medium bowl, cream the butter or margarine with the sugar until it is light and fluffy, then add the melted chocolate, spices, currants, and the poppy seed mixture.

Sift the flour with the baking powder, add it to the bowl, and knead to form a pliable dough. Roll the dough into 24 small balls and put them on a greased cookie sheet, then press them down lightly with a fork.

Bake the cookies at 350°F for 20 minutes until they turn crisp, then allow them to cool on a wire rack.

Top to bottom: Butter Crunch Squares, Chocolate Crescents, and Poppy Seed Cookies

Menu Planners

These menus are intended to help you plan a successful meal. Remember to adjust each individual recipe quantity to suit the number of people you are cooking for.

Greek Menu

(see photograph on pages 108–9)

Melizanasalata (page 24)
served with warmed pita bread

Spanokopitta (page 106)

Potatoes with Lemon (page 129)

Warm Courgette Salad (page 66)

Cephalonian Salad (page 55)

Spiced Fruit Filo Parcels (page 156)
served with Greek yogurt

Italian Menu

Ravioli and Spinach Broth (page 40)

Fontina and Tomato Pie (page 96)

Roasted Mushrooms with
Peperonata (page 135)

Fennel and Arugula Salad (page 50)

Panna Cotta with Raspberry Coulis
(page 166)

Lemon Wafers (page 181)

Mexican Menu

Black Bean Soup (page 42)

Red Enchiladas (page 88) with
Salsa Verde (page 150)

Spicy Corn (page 137)

A simple green salad with avocado
served with Classic Vinaigrette (page 151)
made with lime juice

Sopapillas (page 157)

French Menu

Artichoke, Goat's Cheese, and
Walnut Salad (page 57)

Quiche Linda (page 113)

Fine Beans with Almonds (page 132)

Warm Chocolate Soufflés with
Bittersweet Sauce (page 176)

Spring Menu V

Avocado Hummus (page 22)
served with a
selection of fresh vegetable sticks

....

Asparagus and Lemon Risotto (page 114)

Arugula and Alfalfa Salad (page 66)

....

Rhubarb Fool (page 158)

Summer Menu

Chilled Red Pepper and Lime
Soup (page 42)

....

Pesto Genovese with
Green Beans and Potatoes (page 68)

Surfers' Salad (page 57)

....

Pecan Roulade (page 163)

Autumn Menu V

Vegetable Soup with Coconut (page 38)

....

Chickpea and Okra Stir-fry (page 80)

Grilled Spicy Tofu (page 101)

....

Tarte Tatin (page 173)

Winter Menu

Chilli Corn Fritters (page 24) served with
Garlic Dipping Sauce (page 147)

....

Green Curry (page 102)
served with jasmine, basmati, or
plain boiled rice

....

Pear Flan (page 175)

Menu Planners

(continued)

Birthday Celebration

Baked Portobello Mushrooms (page 77)

Minted Couscous with Roasted Vegetables (page 105)

Lettuce Hearts with Avocado, Croûtons, and Blue Cheese Dressing (page 50)

Fruit Soufflés (page 165)

Pecan Macaroons (page 180)

Children's Party

A selection of sandwiches (page 82–3) and pizza slices (page 116–20)

Savory Puff Pastry Rolls (page 19)

Oven Fries (page 128)

Dishes of cherry tomatoes and a selection of fresh vegetable sticks

Ice Cream Cake (page 158) served with baby bananas and seedless grapes

Chocolate Crescents (page 182)

Easter Menu

Warm Puy Lentils on a Bed of Arugula (page 65)

Traditional Artichoke Pie (page 107)

Mediterranean-style Green Beans (page 142)

Lemon Spinach (page 140)

Naughty Nougat Cake (page 169)

Midsummer's Eve Picnic

Cucumber, Quark, and Dill Soup (page 33)

Caponata (page 23) served with bread sticks

Felafels (page 29) served with Yogurt with Fresh Mint (page 147) and pita bread

Broccoli and Parmesan Tartlets (page 22)

Creole Spinach and Hot Pepper Salad (page 62)

Nutty Wild Rice Salad with Citrus Dressing (page 60)

Fruit Flan (page 156)

Candlelit Dinner

French Onion Soup (page 37)

Asparagus Crêpes with Tarragon and Crème Fraîche (page 20)

Watercress Salad with Mushrooms and Gruyère (page 54)

Non-dairy Crème Brulée (page 178)

Oriental Feast V

(see photograph on pages 72–3)

Spring Rolls (page 30) with Ginger Dipping Sauce (page 146) and Sweet and Sour Chili Dipping Sauce (page 146)

Spicy Tofu (page 71)

Aromatic Vegetable Stir-fry (page 71)

Pad Thai Noodles (page 94)

Special Fried Rice (page 142)

Sweet and Sour Cucumber Salad (page 58)

Crispy Fried Seaweed (page 138)

Toffee Apples and Bananas (page 179)

Coconut Rice Pudding (page 160)

Thanksgiving Meal

Tomato and Rosemary Soup (page 45) served with Croûtons (page 152)

Festive Loaf (page 113)

Herby Stuffing (page 153) served with Special Gravy (page 149)

Oven-roasted Vegetable Fries with Whole Garlic (page 137)

Glazed Carrots with Honey and Sesame Seeds (page 137)

Minted Peas (page 138)

Grandma's Apple Pie (page 161)

Christmas Meal

Broccoli and Stilton Soup (page 36)

Mushroom Roast (page 124) served with Onion and Juniper Gravy (page 151) and Cranberry Sauce (page 148)

Chestnut Stuffing (page 153)

Herby Potato Cakes (page 130)

Brussels Sprouts with Chestnuts (page 141)

Celebration Pudding (page 172) served with Crème Anglaise (page 170)

INDEX

References in bold denote photographs